DEMONOLOGY

THE DEVIL AND THE SPIRITS OF DARKNESS

Possession & Exor‹
(Volume 3)

By

Michael Freze, S., ._

Permission to publish granted at Helena, Montana, by Most Reverend Elden F. Curtiss, former Bishop of Helena. The permission to publish is a statement that the book is free from doctrinal and moral error. No implication is contained therein that the one granting the permission agrees with the contents, opinions, or statements expressed.

The Scripture quotations contained herein are from the New Revised Standard Version Bible: Catholic Edition (Copyright © 1993) by the Division of Christian Education of the National Council of the Churches of Christ in the U.S.A. Used by permission. All rights reserved.

Prologue

Diabolical Oppression

Oppression is the phase by which the evil spirit attempts to take over those present in an environment of diabolical infestation. Now the victim is the object of intense psychological and physical attacks. This period of oppression begins with what is known as diabolical siege, or oppression.

Oftentimes during this phase, more powerful spirits infest the home to intensify the activities and assaults. At this point of demonic infiltration, the victims present are in very serious danger. Once unwilling to reveal himself, the evil spirit now boldly proclaims his identity for what he is: a being intent on an all-out, diabolical assault upon a targeted victim or victims.

Suddenly, a sinister strategy is slowly revealed as the spirit of darkness attempts to take over the unsuspecting victim. The immediate goal is total obsession and, then, perfect possession. The ultimate goal is death of the victim and diabolical victory of the human soul for all eternity. What once may have been dismissed as a series of strange coincidences or flights of the imagination is now unmistakable: Fear has been transformed into diabolical action and replaces it with destruction or harm.

There are two recognizable experiences that occur during this phase: internal oppression and external oppression. **Internal oppression** involves the psychological attack upon the victim. **External oppression** deals with physical attacks upon the body or the senses.

At this point of the siege, mere **deliverance prayer** is rarely successful. Now is the time to call in the services of a Catholic priest. If the obsession continues and proves to be authentic, it is important that the Church approve a **solemn (formal) exorcism** as quickly as possible. If the attempt to rid the evil spirit is too late, partial or perfect possession may have already occurred. When this happens, the victim is in much greater danger, and the exorcism will prove to be more difficult to achieve.

Frightening phenomena are now experienced through the activities of the evil spirit. Such things as materializations, de-materializations, teleportations, apparitions, threatening voices, and exploding objects may begin to take place. A peculiar sign of diabolical obsession is the foul odor of excrement, ozone, or some other stench in the vicinity of the infestation. Frequently, pools of urine may appear throughout an infected environment. Foul or sacrilegious writings may suddenly appear on the walls or ceilings: words that threaten the victim, mock Christ, or ridicule God. If the offensive language is cleaned off the wall, it often reappears suddenly in the exact form it was before.

One of the most frightening experiences that occur during the phase of oppression is the physical manifestation of the evil entity.

The most commonly reported diabolical apparition involves a **Black Mass** that gradually takes the form of a human shape. This Black Mass is often preceded by the sound of a whirling wind; it's as if the entity takes on a visible appearance by drawing in the energy from the environment; particularly, electromagnetic energy from the air and the natural energy that is discharged from the human body. Witnesses have described such a form as blacker than the blackest night.

Once the apparition takes shape and form, it moves toward the victim and attempts to harm him. Sometimes, the apparition appears in the form of a black cat, a snake, a boar, or a hideous-looking creature.

A telltale sign of a demonic apparition is the eerie unnaturalness of the form: There is always something missing or strange about the vision. Perhaps the entity looks like a normal human in every aspect except that it has no eyes. In other cases, the eyes glow or shine in a threatening and piercing manner. Or a fully human-like figure may be missing its head. Most reports indicate that the victim senses something inhuman about the appearance, even though it may not always be grotesque.

Unusual phenomena involving the left side of the senses are common in stages of oppression. For example, there may be only left footprints found outside the home in the snow. Sometimes, a bird is heard singing to the left of one's window, but when investigated, there is no bird to be found. People have reported seeing demonic images out of the corner of the left eye, but when facing the image straight on, it disappears. Finally, others claim to be hit, pulled, scratched, or tugged from the left side of their body, while the right side remains untouched.

Animals are known to be particularly sensitive during the oppression of a home. Pet dogs and cats may begin to hiss or growl at something that humans cannot see. At times, their hair stands on end, even when the animals are sleeping. Farm animals have been known to move around nervously for no apparent reason.

Although one or two people in a family are usually the main targets of diabolical oppression, it can occur to all the family members simultaneously. Unlike cases of poltergeist activity (where the victim is usually a young, adolescent girl with emotional or psychological traumas), diabolical oppression affects males as well as females, and adults as often as children.

Are these phenomena really authentic? As incredible as they may appear, there is in fact a tremendous amount of observable evidence related to these experiences. Literally thousands of photographs exist that depict many preternatural phenomena: levitations of furniture, appliances, and people; pools of urine and piles of feces throughout a home; misty images of diabolical apparitions; unnatural lights that illuminate a room, home, or window; filthy or sacrilegious writings on the wall; spontaneous fires that appear in different places; possessed people who have an inhuman appearance (bloated faces, eyes that seem to be on fire, strange welts on the body, unusually stretched or smooth skin around the face, etc.). Sometimes, inanimate objects such as dolls or toys appear to come alive. There are many cases on record whereby witnesses have seen a doll walk, its eyes and mouth move, and a voice speak from its lips.

Furthermore, numerous tapes exist that have recorded inhuman or diabolical voices. These voices often whine, howl, moan, and screech at decibel levels and pitches not possible for human beings to produce. Animal sounds are mixed with these voices, although no animals were present at the scene. Sometimes the voices speak a foreign language fluently, although no one in the room knew these languages before: Hebrew, Latin, Chinese, English, and a host of other languages have been recorded. Some recordings depict gibberish sounds that seem to make no sense. Yet when the recording is played backward, there is a perfect message in English!

These voices may take on a harsh, gravelly tone that no human can possibly duplicate. This tone is normally a low but piercing sound. Many of these tape recordings have been examined by specialists who have testified that they could not be reproduced or duplicated through any known natural means. A typical example is the male versus female voice. Although oppressive activity may revolve around a male figure, the voices that show up on the recording are of a female character.

Table Of Contents

Dedication

To all members of the Christian faith, who must face the powers of darkness on the journey to Christ. May you remain under God's grace and heed the words of St. Paul to the Ephesians:

Be strong in the Lord and in the strength of his might. Put on the whole armor of God, that you may be able to stand against the wiles of the devil. For we are not contending against flesh and blood, but against the principalities, against the powers, against the world rulers of this present darkness, against the spiritual hosts of wickedness in the heavenly places.Therefore take the whole armor of God, that you may be able to withstand in the evil day, and having done everything, to stand firm (6:10-13).

Acknowledgments

Any work that claims to have a single author is highly misleading and slightly less than honest. This work is no exception.

The truth of the matter is that all books regardless of the topic matter at hand are products of various sources and ideas that originate with different peoples in different places and times. Few ideas are new or original; many are just reworked or given a fresh perspective. This collective consciousness exists in all walks of life, although a few truly original ideas do appear from time to time.

Therefore, I acknowledge my indebtedness to the many sources that helped to make this book a reality. Any oversight on my part is purely unintentional. To all the unsung heroes who make up the collective consciousness of writers past and present, I extend my deepest appreciation.

To Father Patrick G. Patton of the Diocese of Helena, Montana: Thank you for continuing to support my writing career over the years. Father Patton provided encouragement and shared his insights for several of my past works. These include They Bore the Wounds of Christ: The Mystery of the Sacred Stigmata (1989) and The Making of Saints (1991), both published by Our Sunday Visitor.

To the Most Rev. Elden F. Curtiss, former Bishop of Helena and now Archbishop of Omaha: thank you for your encouragement concerning my writing apostolate. As the Ordinary of Helena, Bishop Curtiss was kind enough to take time out of his busy schedule to review this current work.

To Father Joseph Pius Martin, O.F.M. Cap., and Father Alessio Parente, O.F.M. Cap.: I am most grateful for your support and permission to use source materials from Our Lady of Grace Capuchin Friary in San Giovanni Rotondo, Italy. These two dear

Capuchin friars have helped me with my past two works on the stigmata and the saints. Our meetings and interviews at the friary in 1988 and 1990 as well as our ongoing communications have led to a dear friendship that I will always cherish. Father Joseph and Father Alessio lived with the stigmatist Padre Pio (1887-1968) for a number of years before his death. Both served as his daily assistants and companions. Father Joseph Martin was present in Padre Pio's cell when he died.

To the dozens of authors, theologians, and saints throughout the years who have provided excellent works on this most complex of topics: Thank you. Without your previous exhaustive research and reflections, this work would not include the wisdom that you have imparted to all the faithful.

Preface

I decided from the beginning that this work would involve the study of demonology from a Catholic perspective but meant for all faiths. In no way does this book intend to discourage other faiths or denominations from studying its contents. Indeed, I made use of a number of credible expert sources from non-Catholic traditions for some of my information. But by and large, I had decided to write this work principally from a Catholic perspective. Why?

For one thing, there are few recent works on demonology in the Catholic market that treat the topic in an in-depth, historical, and critical manner. The few works that do exist are usually focused on one particular case, person, or phenomenon. Oftentimes these works are sensational in nature, a weakness I have tried to keep to a minimum.

Secondly, there are already many books on demonology in the Protestant markets. The Catholic market needs to devote some attention to this topic as well. Although there are many fine works on demonology in the Protestant field (indeed, it must be admitted that Protestant scholars have studied this phenomenon much more closely these past decades than Catholics as a whole). Nevertheless, there remains a serious drawback to most of these works in print.

Many of the popular works on demonology stem from fundamentalist and evangelical denominations. One of the problems associated with these works (at least for Catholics) is that they tend to emphasize a personal combat with evil forces that isolates these experiences from the authority and witness of the universal Church. Their Bible only theology and the personal relationship with God perspective separate the timeless, cosmic dimension of the spiritual warfare and also place this mystery of iniquity within the realm (and control) of private individuals who believe they possess a spiritual gift to cure all ills. To say that this fundamental, isolationist approach to the treatment of diabolical oppression or possession is wrong would be to understate the issue.

It must be clearly understood that the Catholic Church believes that the ongoing spiritual battle between the forces of darkness and light is essentially a cosmic conflict that only God can control through His own direct power or through the authority He commissions to His universal Church.

This Church, when acting under the name and authority of Jesus Christ, represents all true believers of the faith. In turn, some are appointed who have been delegated authority to act for the Church in a solemn, formal manner. This authoritative structure is no small matter. Rather, the Church sees a special grace given to those ecclesiastical authorities who are considered successors of the original Apostles: namely, the bishops of the world. In turn, those the bishops appoint are given special graces to deal with the evil spirit in a confident, powerful manner.

Christ Himself promised special protection and power over the spirits of darkness for those whom He particularly calls: You did not choose me, but I chose you (Jn 15:16). In the Catholic Church, Christ commissions this work. He delegates His own authority through the ecclesiastical office of the Apostolic successors.

This chain of command or delegation of authority is precisely what is lacking in many fundamentalist and evangelical denominations. Yet Christ Himself makes is very clear that this is the will of God the Father. Even the Son is delegated authority through His Father: He who believes in me, believes not in me, but in him who sent me.. . . For I have not spoken on my own authority; the Father who sent me has himself given me commandment what to say and what to speak. And know that his commandment is eternal life. What I say, therefore, I say as the Father has bidden me (Jn 12:44-50).

In light of this revelation, it is difficult to understand how some of these religious groups justify their Bible only, personal relationship only positions concerning their faith life and theology. It is true that some are given personal charisms for particular benefits of the Church: Now there are a variety of gifts, but the same Spirit (1 Cor 12:4). But Jesus also taught us that when a special gift is used for the benefit of others in the universal Church, proper authority must be given to exercise such charisms in the name and authority of the Church: And he called to him his twelve disciples and gave them authority over unclean spirits, to cast them out, and to heal every disease and every infirmity (Mt 10:1; emphasis mine).

Oftentimes, many religious groups believe in their own authority through direct access to God; they do not subscribe to Apostolic succession or authority, nor do they believe in a hierarchical structure. Yet Jesus claimed that even in the world of faith, there indeed exists a hierarchical structure that all must respect: disciple is not above his teacher, nor a servant above his master; it is enough for the disciple to be like his teacher, and the servant like his master (Mt 10:24-25). Or again: He who receives you receives me, and he who receives me receives him who sent me (Mt 10:40).

Apostolic authority is as old as the Gospel itself. Yet many refuse to acknowledge such an authority! Jesus made the point clear in Matthew 16:18-19: And I tell you, you are Peter, and on this rock I will build my church, and the powers of death shall not prevail against it. I will give you the keys of the kingdom of heaven, and whatever you bind on earth shall be bound in heaven, and whatever you loose on earth shall be loosed in heaven.

Perhaps this explanation helps to clear up any misunderstandings that both Catholics and non-Catholics might have concerning the way the Church perceives her mission and duties regarding the battle against the evil spirit. It should be clear that there are fundamental differences in approaching the study of demonology between Catholics and others, especially in the actions taken against the evil spirit himself. Authority plays a crucial role in successfully dealing with the spirits of darkness, especially in the name and power of Jesus Christ. This we all can agree upon.

However, the Catholic Church believes that this very authority is not a private undertaking or venture. Rather, the authority of Jesus Christ is transmitted to others by virtue of the collective authority of the magisterium of the Church.

It is true that so-called deliverance prayer (a type of informal, private exorcism) is allowed to be practiced by certain Catholics experienced and knowledgeable in such matters. Indeed, we are all encouraged to resist the devil (Jas 4:7). This concerns efforts to combat demonic temptations, infiltrations, obsessions, etc. But for the more serious diabolical attacks such as with total oppression, partial possession, or complete possession deliverance prayer may not only be inadvisable; it may also be quite dangerous to the innocent victim who attempts to deal with the evil spirit on his or her own.

In such extreme situations, a formal exorcism may be in order. This type of expulsion of the evil spirit is a solemn public act, one that carries the authority of the universal Church behind it. It is Christ exercising His greatest power through His collective Body:
The church is subject to Christ (Eph 5:24). St. Paul had pointed this out quite well: For the body does not consist of one member but many. . . Now you are the body of Christ and individually members of it (1 Cor 12:14, 27).

As far as understanding God's will, it is also through the authoritative structure of the Church that we find our best teacher, director, and guide when combating the forces of darkness. It is dangerous to attempt a confrontation with the inhuman spirit without the aid of the collective wisdom and mighty grace of the Church: Through the church the manifold wisdom of God might now be made known to the principalities and powers in the heavenly places. This was according to the eternal purpose which he has realized in
Christ Jesus our Lord (Eph 3:10-11; emphasis mine).

Note that Paul does not restrict our God-given knowledge and powers to individuals for the sake of individuals; rather, God uses individual charisms through the authority of the Church for the benefit of its members. Anything other than that would be self-serving and could open the door for diabolical intervention and control.

Thus, with this preface I have intended to point out the different perspective one finds in the study of demonology from a Catholic point of view. As we have seen, this difference is important to note when considering the various theologies about demonology that exist throughout the Christian and non-Christian world.

This is not to say that the Catholic position is the only correct one; on the contrary, we all have much to learn from each other. But in any given field of study, one must start from a particular point of reference and remain true to the general principles of that particular view. Only then will one be able to express a viewpoint that is consistent and readily identifiable among the audience for which the work is intended. I hope that I have
achieved this purpose for the reader.

Introduction

Belief in the existence of the devil and various demonic forces has fascinated, mystified, and terrified the faithful since the beginning of human history. Despite what is sometimes called a morbid interest, little is known about the world of demonology except for the material gathered by those who have devoted themselves to studying this particular branch of spiritual theology. This usually includes various priests, nuns, theologians, mystics, saints, and Doctors of the Church.

Many have come to know the reality of the spirits of darkness through personal experience: those who have been oppressed or possessed, ecclesiastically appointed exorcists or their assistants, first-hand witnesses or victims of paranormal phenomena, etc.

What exactly is demonology? How does this term differ from other studies in the Christian faith? One thing that it is not is a practice that involves conjuring spirits, telecommunications, mental telepathy, psychic phenomena, seances, and so forth. Although modern investigations do make use of other disciplines in the study of demonology, the above particular phenomena are subject to the scientific discipline known as paranormal psychology. (The use of parapsychology and all its aspects will be discussed at greater length later on in this work.)

Parapsychology is a field to be respected. I only wish to emphasize that these studies are used to help explain all phenomena that may not be the result of authentic diabolical activity. Thus, it is important to consider all disciplines that might reveal a natural or reasonable cause for actions too often presumed to be the work of the devil.

The main point is that although one studies and takes seriously these other fields such as parapsychology, no one encourages dabbling with the occult merely for curiosity. This must be kept in mind for all serious students involved with the modern study of demonology and all its ramifications.

To observe, study, and consider frequently requires a multidisciplinary approach. To perform experiments in the presence of experts (and with the proper permission and authority to do so!) is often necessary in order to identify a reasonable cause or effect.

Beyond that, it is a dangerous game to dabble with unseen forces or to attempt communications with spirits for the sake of innocent curiosity or amusement.

Above all, I want to set the record straight on this point: Do not do these things out of morbid curiosity! Leave this work to those experts who are commissioned by the authorities of the Church to do so. To ignore this advice is to open the door to potential danger.

Demonology may be defined as that theological discipline involving the study of all phenomena related to evil spirits: their creation, essence, substance, and interaction in the cosmic world. A demonologist studies the types and roles of evil spirits, their will, intelligence, power, and interaction with human beings. A demonologist is also concerned with the cosmic (or spiritual) battle between the forces of good and the forces of evil: the fall of Satan; the role of Michael the Archangel; the Antichrist; and the climactic encounter at the end of time.

This discipline examines preventive measures to use as protection against the spirits of darkness, as well as the treatments used for those already under attack from the evil spirit. Various signs and degrees of diabolical interaction are also dealt with in demonology: signs of temptation, infiltration, obsession, and oppression; deliverance prayer and ministry; informal and formal exorcism; and so forth.

Demonology may properly be called a specialized field of study within the discipline known as spiritual theology. This field must not be confused with angelology, which is reserved for the study of the heavenly angels: the archangels, the choirs of angels, guardian angels, and so on. Although both disciplines require an extensive understanding of all angelic creatures, nevertheless the primary focus of each one is separate and distinct.

Spiritual theology embraces a wide variety of specialized disciplines: demonology, angelology, prayer, spiritual direction, mystical theology, and aesthetic theology, to name but a few. Even moral theology may be considered so intimately bound to the spiritual or interior life that many consider this a sub-branch of spiritual theology.

Although the roots of demonology predate the existence of Christianity itself, our own century has witnessed a revival of interest in this mysterious topic. Indeed, the twentieth century as a whole and particularly the time since the early 1970s has been a period of revival unprecedented since the early Middle Ages. Particularly fascinating to some people today are the reported cases of possession and exorcism.

Although admittedly a rare phenomenon, diabolic possession has been a subject studied closely by the Catholic Church. Not so rare are the diabolical temptations, infiltrations, and even oppressions that continually plague the lives of individuals.

In order to deal with the cases of authentic oppression and possession that came before the Church throughout the centuries, it was agreed by Rome that there should be a formal, written guide as to the methods and procedures to be used concerning an authorized, formal exorcism. Created in 1614, this guide, known as the Rituale Romanum (Roman Ritual), was implemented during the pontificate of Pope Paul V (1605-1621). The Rituale Romanum includes the rite of exorcism that each appointed exorcist uses.

Indeed, the Church takes this reality so seriously that she has even stated her formal position in the magisterial document of post-Vatican II: Les formes multiples de la superstition (Christian

Faith and Demonology, Sacred Congregation for Divine Worship, June 26, 1975).

On November 15, 1972, in his General Address, Pope Paul VI had this to say about the reality of the spirits of darkness: Evil is not merely the lack of something, but an effective agent, a living, spiritual being, perverted and perverting. A terrible reality. Mysterious and frightening. It is contrary to the teaching of the Bible and the Church to refuse to recognize the existence of such a reality. . . , or to explain it as a pseudo-reality, a conceptual and fanciful personification of the unknown causes of our misfortunes. The Devil was a murderer from the beginning . . . and the father of lies, as Christ defines him (John 8:44-45); he launches sophistic attacks on the moral equilibrium of man. . . .

Not that every sin is directly attributable to diabolical action; but it is true that those who do not watch over themselves with a certain moral strictness (cf. Mt 12:45; Eph 6:11) are exposed to the influence of the 'mysterium iniquitatis' to which St. Paul refers (2 Thes 2:3-12) and run the risk of being damned (L'Osservatore Romano, November 23, 1972).

The cause of such revival is not too difficult to detect. In our modern era of television, radio, and the print media, the sensational topics are accessible to every home throughout the civilized world. Curiosity provided by a massive influx through the media begins a wave of interest that then sustains itself. Another factor contributing to the recent interest concerning the devil or demons is the obsession with Satanism and witchcraft. This interest has increased dramatically throughout the world.

Oftentimes, members of these cults identify with drugs and alcohol, which further influence their imaginations and contribute to their lack of inhibitions. This is particularly true in those areas of life that call for moral decisions and actions that normally guide our thoughts and conscience as individuals and as a society. Drugs can alter those inhibitive feelings, opening up the door to innocent exploring and dabbling with the occult. Naturally, this produces an invitation for diabolical intrusion at some deeper point of one's involvement.

Satanism, sorcery, witchcraft, black magic these have all been with us for centuries. Yet the increased use of psychoactive-psychedelic drugs is at an all-time high, creating a virtual cesspool of naive and confused people who look for something bigger and better in order to find meaning and fulfillment in their lives. Drugs and alcohol can be effective catalysts for those who are young, confused, and curious. They can also be open invitations to the lures of the devil.

Anton LaVey, founder and high priest of San Francisco's First Church of Satan, once claimed that the Satanic Age began in 1966. His own books, The Satanic Bible (1969) and The Satanic Rituals (1972), both published by Avon Books, have sold in the thousands. And no wonder. Statistics report that in France alone there are more than sixty thousand sorcerers earning two hundred thousand dollars per year for their services. In another report, it was said that six thousand witches meet on a regular basis to perform their rituals in England.

Perhaps the most influence regarding modern-day fascination with demonology is generated through books and through television. The real mass, or popular, revival concerning an interest in demonology began with the William P. Blatty novel The Exorcist (first published in 1971). Although the novel used a twelve-year-old girl named Regan MacNeil as the possessed victim of the story, this novel was based upon the real-life story of Douglass Deen, a thirteen-year-old possessed boy from the Washington, D.C., suburb of Mount Rainier. Deen allegedly experienced a number of poltergeist phenomena between January and May of 1949; he was also the victim of obscene diabolical gestures, physical attacks, obsession, and complete possession.

It is claimed that the Deens' Lutheran pastor attempted to free the boy from diabolical attacks but to no avail. After accompanying the boy through unsuccessful medical and psychiatric evaluations at Georgetown Hospital and at the hospital at St. Louis University (both Jesuit institutions), the Jesuits took official control of the situation.

In due time, Deen was helped by a Jesuit priest in his fifties. This priest was formally commissioned by the Church to perform the exorcism. Although the exorcism was successful, it took thirty separate attempts over a six-month period to complete the ordeal. The exorcist eventually retired in St. Louis. In a strange twist of fate, Douglass Deen like William Peter Blatty attended Georgetown University. He later married and raised a family. In 1949, this extraordinary story was well-known to William Peter Blatty, a Catholic student at Georgetown University in Washington, D.C. He would live with this experience for several decades before committing his story to print.

Following the phenomenal success of the book, The Exorcist was made into a movie (1972). Its director, William Friedkin, once interviewed the seventy-two-year-old aunt of the boy who was eventually exorcised of his demons. On August 27, 1972, The New York Times reviewed the film. The reviewer, Chris Chase, interviewed Douglass Deen's aunt concerning the real story behind the movie. Many terrifying phenomena were explained in that interview: poltergeist activity, shaking beds, a mattress that rose in the air, etc. According to the aunt, this all occurred one day when Douglass Deen had visited her home before the exorcism.

Another film that opened the doors of public curiosity is Rosemary's Baby, a 1966 motion picture that depicts a young actor who makes a pact with a group of Satanists. In turn, this group is given permission to use the actor's wife as the bride of Satan in order that evil might be introduced into the world. As a reward for such sacrifices, the young actor is promised wealth and success.

More recently, a book called The Amityville Horror by Jay Anson rocked the nation with its story of a terrorized family (the Lutzes) who live in a possessed Long Island home. Apparently, the house was originally built on an Indian burial ground. Having been disturbed in the past, it is claimed that demonic spirits took over the residence. It is also claimed that in the late 1600s, John Ketchum, expelled from Salem, Massachusetts, for practicing witchcraft, lived on the spot where this 1928 Dutch Colonial home now stands. In November of 1974, a story reports that twenty-two-year-old Ronald DeFeo killed his entire family with a .35 caliber rifle in this house, claiming that Satan made him do it. All told, Ronald's parents, his two brothers, and two sisters died that night.

From December 18, 1975, to January 7, 1976, George and Kathy Lutz lived in the haunted home. The Lutzes experienced a multitude of paranormal phenomena from unseen forces, including the following: poltergeist activity; foul smells throughout the house; demonic visions; scratchings in the walls; unexplained temperature changes; cold spots in the house; blood oozing from the walls; and violent, physical attacks from unseen forces. Needless to say, the Lutzes left their new home after only twenty days.

Dozens of parapsychologists, scientists, and ecclesiastical figures investigated the home; extensive interviews were also held with the Lutzes. The story remains controversial, as some of the experts confirm the authenticity of the reported events and some do not. Since that time, a number of Amityville sequels have hit the markets. Several successful movies have been made from the original books as well.

It is obvious that such media coverage attracts public attention and causes unprecedented interest in such reported cases. Although a great deal of these stories are sensationalized, many are certainly not true; nevertheless it must be acknowledged that some of them have to be authentic. There have been too many of these paranormal experiences reported to dismiss them outright. There is simply too much credible evidence from professional authorities (not to mention countless eyewitnesses) who swear by the observations they have experienced.

In light of this fact, the reader needs to keep an open mind about such reported incidences. A healthy approach is a cautious one: Doubt each case until the evidence is very convincing, but do not deny every reported incident out of hand. This would be a tragic mistake, for the Church demands that we believe in the reality of Satan, the demons, and their ability to interact in our lives.

The evil spirit would love nothing more than for the faithful to believe that he does not exist. The devil tries to disguise his actions lest he be caught. To ruin the lives of many and to capture souls away from the kingdom of God without being acknowledged allows him to carry on his tactics unopposed. Remember the words of St. Paul: Even Satan disguises himself as an angel of light (2 Cor 11:14).

One final thing: It cannot be emphasized enough that many of the supernatural apparitions and messages contained in this work have not yet received official approval of the Church, and are still under ecclesiastical investigation. Therefore, the reader must realize that these claims are not necessarily the beliefs or opinions of the author or publisher, nor are they intended to be an official position of the Church.

Possession

Partial Possession

Demonic possession may be defined as the inner control or takeover of the body by Satan himself, another devil, or a demonic spirit. This is the last phase in a **diabolical siege** whereby the demon attempts to gain complete dominance of a human being. Demonic possession has always been recognized by the Church as a possibility, learning her wisdom from the example of Christ, who Himself confronted possessed persons (see Mk 5:1-20).

In the previous **Code of Canon Law** (1917), the Church was very clear in her teachings about the reality of the devil, obsessions, possessions, and the occasional need for a formal exorcism. In fact, three different canons specifically dealt with these phenomena:

Canon 1151: No one, even though qualified to act as an exorcist, may proceed to the exorcism of possessed persons without the special and explicit permission of his ordinary (that is, his bishop).

The bishop will not grant this permission except to a priest known to be pious, prudent, and of irreproachable conduct; and the priest will not undertake the exorcism until it has been adequately established, after cautious and careful examination, that the subject to be exorcised is really possessed by the devil.

Canon 1152: Exorcisms practiced by authorized ministers may be undertaken not only for the faithful and for catechumens but also for non-Catholics and the excommunicated.

Canon 1153: Those who are authorized to employ the exorcisms used in baptism, consecrations, and benedictions are the legitimate ministers of these sacred rites.

Many saints in the history of the Church have claimed belief in the possibility of demonic possession. St. Paulinus (d. 358), Bishop of Trier and companion of St. Athanasius (297-373), once believed that he saw a possessed man walk to the arch of a church, his head bent downward, completely naked. The victim was later cured at the tomb. of St. Felix of Nola (d. c. 260).

St. Jerome (342-420), Doctor of the Church, gave us many examples of what he believed to be diabolical possession. In one story, Jerome claims that Paula heard the voices of many devils at the tomb of St. John the Baptist (first century). Paula described these demonic sounds as howlings, barkings, and whistlings. Other preternatural phenomena such as bodily levitations were witnessed near the tomb.

The great St. Hilarion (291-371), desert monk and friend of St. Antony of Egypt (251-356), described many cases of possessed people who were brought to his attention. In one example, Hilary confronts a possessed camel that foamed at the mouth and roared in a frightening manner.

Possessions may be involuntary, whereby a person is overcome through unconscious desires to communicate with the dead (spiritualistic mediums, shamanistic practices, etc.), or by innocent attempts to play games or explore the unknown (such as playing with a Ouija board, tarot cards, or reading tea leaves. It can also be voluntary, occurring through the deliberate and conscious decision to invoke the aid of demons.

Those who practice the occult, Satanism, witchcraft, and so on open themselves up to the domination of an evil spirit. Likewise, those who cast spells, charms, practice black magic or **white magic** (so-called **gray witchcraft**) voluntarily submit to the possibility of a diabolical takeover. The casting of a spell known as a **malefice** is a common cause of diabolical persecution.

Sortilege, another term for an act of sorcery, often produces cases of diabolical possession. This practice is very ancient and is still observed in primitive tribes or cultures throughout the world. The sorcerer is believed to have supernatural gifts that allow him to control illness, natural forces, and signs in the sky.

Traditionally, there are good sorcerers and bad ones: the latter performing charms or spells upon a victim through superstitious ceremonies. Oftentimes, the devil uses such acts as a gateway to enter and control an unsuspecting victim.

Possessions can be continuous or intermittent, singular or multiple. Possession is usually not the end goal of the evil spirit; rather, there is one more final step it desires: physical death and eternal damnation of the soul.

In turn, demonic possession is broken down into two distinct phases: **partial (imperfect) possession** and **perfect (complete) possession**. The former involves a diabolical control of the inner person who still retains some freedom of will. In this state, the victim's possession is often expressed intermittently there are still moments (of brief or long duration) whereby the possessed regains his faculties and appears to think and act in a normal manner.

With perfection possession, the diabolical domination is usually continuous and quite severe. Rarely (if ever) does the demon retrieve from the possessed. When perfect possession has been achieved, the victim may or may not survive. When things are this grim, only a formal exorcism sanctioned by the Church can free the victim from his or her crisis. Although many argue that even during possession a person still retains freedom of will, this in fact may not always be the case. Because perfect possession is quite rare, it is important to distinguish the two distinct phases of diabolical possession.

In cases of partial possession, the victim may or may not know that he or she has been taken over by an unclean spirit. Some have reported that they are fully conscious and aware of what is happening, yet unable to do anything about it. Others claim that when the possession is in remission, they do not recall anything about their domination by an inhuman spirit. In most cases of perfect possession, the victim rarely knows of his or her state, since the domination is so complete that the demon and the victim become as one.

Perfect Possession

Perfect possession is a rare phenomenon in the life of the Church. One noted Parisian priest claimed that he never once encountered an authentic case of total possession in his forty as diocesan exorcist. Although authentic cases are rare, this does not mean that they are nonexistent. Many other priests appointed as diocesan exorcists have claimed otherwise.

It must be acknowledged that true possession never involves any type of animation; that is, the demon can never take the place of the soul of a victim, nor does he give life to the body. Rather, the demon is able to manipulate the actions of the body and dominate the personality of the possessed. The spirit a divine creation is never manipulated or changed directly by the demon who possesses. Although it appears to be so, it is only a diabolical illusion. The devil can only take complete possession of a soul after death if the victim had knowingly and deliberately rejected God without a true and honest repentance during the course of one's life.

By manipulating the body of the possessed, the demon may appear to look out of the eyes of the victim and to speak through his or her mouth. In some cases, many devils or demons possess a victim at the same time. When this occurs, it is known as a **multiple possession**. Encounters with such phenomena reveal that every diabolical spirit has a separate and unique personality, intelligence, and duty.

Likewise, not all demonic spirits are of equal power: The weaker diabolical spirit is the demon, and the stronger one a devil. This hierarchical structure is often revealed during a formal exorcism. Satan, or the devil, is at the top of the **diabolical hierarchical order**, followed by numerous assistant devils and then the lower class of evil spirits.

Even so, the weakest evil spirit is much stronger and far more intelligent than any human being. To take lightly an unclean spirit who reveals that he is of a lower order would be both foolish and dangerous. Without the protection of God's grace and the authority of the Church, the individual who goes it alone or defies such a demonic being through mere self-confidence may very well discover that the evil spirit can cause serious harm or death to one who challenges or confronts such an entity under false pretenses.

Signs of Authentic Possession

What are the signs that the Church looks for in a case of authentic possession? Are there indications that preclude a diabolical influence or domination?

According to the **Roman Ritual**, several signs are indicative of an alien intelligence:

1. When the victim speaks in an unknown language or understands those who speak it.

2. When the person can reveal distant or hidden events and things.

3. If the victim shows a strength beyond the normal human capacity, allowing for his age and constitution.

4. If the victim suspends the laws of nature, such as when one levitates above the ground, floats to the ceiling, or walks upside down on a ceiling or a wall.

5. When the alleged possessed shows a violent reaction to prayer, holy water, relics, a crucifix, or anything that is religious in nature.

Other signs have been noted as well, including the following:

1. Convulsions, displaying an intelligence foreign to that of the patient, and frequent alterations of normal and abnormal states.

2. Extraordinary movements that could not be produced without long practice, such as jumping, dancing, balancing feats, complicated creeping movements, blows, wounds, falls without

apparent cause, twisting of the neck, etc.

3. Distortions or intolerable pain immediately relieved by the application of holy water, the Sign of the Cross, a blessed wafer, etc.

4. Sudden loss of sense and feelings, immediately restored by conjuration.

5. Animal or strange howlings, of which the patient is unconscious in the sense that he does not remember them afterward.

6. Strange and demonic visions in an otherwise normal person.

7. Sudden and violent rages caused by the sight of sacred objects or of a priest, or on passing a church when a companion wishes to enter it.

8. Unable to swallow or retain blessed foods or drinks (The Mystical State and the Extraordinary Facts of Spiritual Life).

Cases of Diabolical Possession

The Medieval World of Lyons (1526): case reported where several nuns were possessed and later exorcised.

Wertet (1550): In the county of Hoorn, Brabant, several nuns gave a poor woman three pounds of salt, receiving six in return. Soon thereafter, the nuns began climbing the trees like wild animals, invisibly pinched and beaten by unseen hands, and levitated several feet into the air. It is claimed that a local woman had bewitched the nuns at the convent.

Kentorp (1552): In this town located near Strasbourg, a group of nuns reportedly were freed from possession when Elizabeth Kama, the cook, had been forced to confess that she was a witch, as was her mother.

Rome (1554): It was reported that eighty-two women, who were converted Jews, became possessed through the curses made upon them by their angry relatives for having abandoned their Jewish faith. Pope Paul IV attempted to banish all the Jews but was dissuaded.

Rome (1555): A local orphanage claimed that eighty children had become possessed.

Xante (1560): Several nuns in this town of Spain were seen behaving hysterically in church, tearing off their veils and going into convulsions.

Cologne (1565): At a Nazareth convent, a group of nuns were accused of having affairs with various men. They claimed that their sin was due to evil spirits, who frequently appeared to them as dogs.

Laon (1566): Madame Nicole Autry was exorcised by being whipped at Laon, France, by a group of local monks. Autry was accused of allowing the devil into her body. King Charles IX was a witness to the exorcism.

Amsterdam (1566): Thirty boys were claimed to be possessed in a local hospital. During the exorcism, witnesses saw them vomiting needles, pieces of cloth, hair, and glass.

Odernheim on Rhine (1577): Devilish dogs were blamed for haunting several nuns during the night. The Sisters claimed that these dogs attempted to seduce them while soft music played in their presence.

Vienna (1583): A sixteen-year-old girl was accused of being possessed, showing typical signs of demonic phenomena. It was claimed that the exorcism took eight weeks to complete, and that the local Jesuits had expelled 12,652 demons from her body!

Mons (1585): It was reported that the Archbishop of Cambrai exorcised Sister Jeanne Fery.

Amiens (1586): A young girl was accused of being possessed by King Henry III of France. The girl's mother claimed that she had terrible sores that came at the time of her menstruation. It was later found that the young girl suffered from a case of gonorrhea. She was publicly whipped at Amiens when the community found that she had faked being possessed once before in the past.

Milan (1590): Reports of mass hysteria claimed as thirty nuns were found to be possessed.

Paris (1598): Marthe Brossier claimed to be possessed. The local Capuchin monks believed it was a genuine case, but the doctors who examined her disagreed. Bishop Miron of Angers also claimed she was fraudulent.

Aix-en-Provence (1611): Father Louis Gaufridi was accused of bewitching two Sisters in this French city. The priest was later tortured and burned for his heretical practice, and the two nuns were expelled from their convent.

Lille (1613): Three nuns accused a Marie de Sains of bewitching them. Witnesses heard the nuns speak in tongues, and rumors suggested that the women engaged in sexual pleasures: On Mondays and Tuesdays, they reportedly copulated; on Thursdays, they engaged in acts of sodomy; it is also reported that these nuns were frequently involved in homosexual activities. On Saturdays, the nuns were accused of strange practices with dogs, cats, goats, and winged serpents. Then on Wednesday and Fridays, they sang litanies to the devil. One of the witnesses to this strange phenomenon was Father Francis Domptius, the exorcist of the case.

Auxonne (1622): Three bishops and five physicians claimed that the local convent was possessed. When Sister Denise was investigated, the doctor stuck needles under her fingernails. Because she showed no signs of pain, it was concluded that the nuns had been bewitched. Later on, several local women were accused of doing the bewitching. Subsequently, they were lynched by a large mob.

Madrid (1628): A group of nuns was reported to be possessed by the members of the Spanish Inquisition.

Loudun (1634): The Mother Superior of a convent in this French town showed signs of diabolical possession. The case of possessions spread throughout various convents, resulting in the accusation of a Father Urbain Grandier (enemy of Cardinal Richelieu) of bewitching the nuns and who was consequently burned at the stake.

Chinon (1640): A series of possessions and exorcisms were reported. It is said that a priest had raped a young woman on the altar. In addition, stains on the altar cloth were found to be from the blood of a sacrificed chicken. A Father Baure, who had been an exorcist at Loudon, performed the same duties at Chinon. He was later accused of falsifying the story about the priest and was subsequently banished from the area through the orders of the Archbishop of Lyons.

Louviers (1642): Eighteen nuns were reportedly possessed through the bewitchment caused by a Sister Madeleine Bavent and a Father Boulle. In 1647, Father Boulle was accused and burned at the stake.

Paderborn (1656): A number of Capuchin friars were accused of practicing sorcery. Upon further investigation, it was discovered that a maid of a certain burgomaster was the culprit in the case. Several items were found in the maid's possession: a toad, pieces of hair, needles, etc. It was claimed that the entire diocese reported cases of diabolical oppression and possession during this time.

Mora (1669): This town of Sweden experienced an epidemic of mass hysteria among numerous children, who reportedly had hallucinations concerning a sabbat.

Hoorn (1670): In this Holland village, all children under twelve years old in an orphanage were claimed to be possessed.

Toulouse (1681): A report accused Marie Clauzette and four other novices of being possessed. They were subsequently exorcised, even though the local courts eventually found the girls to be impostors.

Salem (1682): This town of Massachusetts is the only American case of mass epidemic reports of bewitchment and diabolical possession.

Lyons (1687): There were reports of mass hysteria and diabolical possession of fifty nuns here.

Lyons (1691): A Marie Volet claimed that she was possessed. Upon investigation, Doctor Rhodes and Canon d'Estaing of Lyons thought that Marie was a fake. She was subsequently placed in a home for the mentally ill.

Les Landes (1744): A number of girls were exorcised by Father Heurtin. The girls showed signs of being possessed, and they claimed to feel they were under the domination of the devil.

Unterzeil (1749): This town of Lower Franconia claimed that several of their nuns had been possessed for years, exhibiting signs of diabolical phenomena: convulsions, swellings, delirium, etc. The sub-prioress, Maria Renata, was later burned as a witch.

Amiens (1816): A pregnant girl claimed to be possessed, saying that three demons had invaded her body: Mimi, Zozo, and Crapoulet. During the exorcism by a local Jesuit priest, Mimi left quickly,
Zozo broke windows in the church before departing, and Crapoulet refused to be expelled. Because he was unsuccessful at casting out the last demon, the Jesuit priest was forbidden to perform another exorcism on the girl.

Exorcism

Deliverance

Catholic Exorcism: A Brief Background

Exorcism is the act of driving, or warding off, demons, or evil spirits, from persons, places, or things, that are, or are believed to be, possessed or infested by these spirits. In the Roman Catholic Church, the means employed for this purpose is the name of God (Jesus Christ) through the power and authority of His Church.

The word exorcism is itself not biblical. Rather, it is derived from the word **exorcisto**, which is used in the Septuagint (Gn 24:3), where it means cause to swear: And I will make you swear by the Lord.

In 1 Kings 22:16, it is used for **adjure**. The latter usage can also be found in Matthew 26:63: I adjure you by the living God, tell us if you are the Christ, the Son of God, as well as in Acts 19:13: I adjure you by the Jesus whom Paul preaches.The noun exorkistes (exorcist) occurs in the Acts of the Apostles:Then some of the itinerant Jewish exorcists undertook to pronounce the name of the Lord Jesus over those who had evil spirits (Acts 19:13).

Adjuration is a term frequently used by Catholic theologians to describe the actual expulsion (exorcism) of the evil spirit. Literally, adjure means to charge solemnly under oath, or to ask earnestly. Thus, the demon is commanded to leave in the power and authority of the name Jesus Christ.

Exorcism is a strictly religious act or rite. But in ethnic religions, and even among the Jews from the time when there is evidence of its being in vogue, exorcism as an act of religion is largely replaced by the use of mere magical and superstitious means, to which non-Catholic writers sometimes unfairly assimilate Christian exorcism.

Superstition should not be equated with religion, however much their history may be interwoven, nor magic, however white it may be, with a legitimate religious rite. There is no instance in the Old Testament of demons being expelled by men. In the Book of Tobit, it is an angel who took the devil and cast him into the desert of upper Egypt: And the demon smelled the odor and fled to the remotest parts of Egypt, and the angel bound him (Tb 8:3).

In extracanonical Jewish literature there are incantations for exorcising demons, examples of which may be seen in the Talmud (Shabbath 19:3; Aboda Zara 12:2; Sanhedrin 10:1). These were sometimes inscribed on the interior surface of earthen bowls, a collection of which is preserved in the Royal Museum in Berlin. These inscriptions (estimated to be from the seventh century A.D.) have been translated.

The chief characteristic of these Jewish exorcisms is their naming of names (believed to be efficacious), such as the names of good angels, which are used either alone or in combination with El (God). The reliance on mere names had long become a superstition with the Jews, and it was considered most important that the appropriate names should be used. It was partly superstition that prompted the sons of Sceva, who had witnessed St. Paul's successful exorcisms in the name of Jesus, to try on their own account the formula (see Acts 19:13).

It was a popular Jewish belief that Solomon had received the power of expelling demons, and that he had composed and transmitted certain formulas that were effective for that purpose.

The Jewish historical records indicates that Eleazar, in the presence of the Emperor Vespasian and his officers, successfully exorcised a demon through the nostril of a possessed person by applying a magical ring surrounded with special roots to the individual's nose.

In what appears to be a superstitious or magical belief, Scripture reveals the Jews felt that demons could be cast out by the power of Beelzebub: Then a blind and dumb demoniac was brought to him, and he healed him, so that the dumb man spoke and saw. And all the people were amazed, and said, `Can this be the Son of David?' But when the Pharisees heard it they said, `It is only by Beelzebub, the prince of demons, that this man casts out demons' (Mt 12:22-24). A bit later in the same Gospel, the Pharisees and the scribes asked Jesus to see a sign. Knowing the superstitious character of these people, Jesus replied: An evil and adulterous generation seeks for a sign (Mt 12:38-39).

In the New Testament, there is an extraordinary amount of evidence indicating that exorcism was an act that was frequently performed, especially by Jesus Himself. Jesus appealed to His power over demons as one of the recognized signs of Messiahship (Mt 12:23, 28; Lk 11:20). He cast out demons, He declared, by the finger or spirit of God, not, as His adversaries alleged, by a secret agreement with the prince of demons (Mt 12:24, 27; Mk 3:22; Lk 11:15, 19).

That He exercised no mere delegated power but a personal authority that was properly His own is clear from the direct and imperative way in which He commands the demons to depart (Mk 9:24-25). Oftentimes, it was only a word which Jesus spoke that successfully expelled a demon: That evening they brought to him many who were possessed with demons; and he cast out the spirits with a word, and healed all who were sick (Mt 8:16).

In many instances, Christ performed the exorcism at a distance (Mt 15:22; Mk 7:25). The demons revealed that they recognized the Son of God (Mk 1:24), and feared that He had come to punish them before their appointed time (see Mt 8:29; Lk 8:28).

It has often been assumed that for the people of the primitive Church, possession was really nothing more than an unknown but physically based disease. Yet Jesus clearly distinguishes between the two. In Luke's Gospel, we have the following statement that supports such a distinction: And he said to them, `Go and tell that fox, Behold, I cast out demons and perform cures today and tomorrow" (Lk 13:32). Note the word and used to identify the reality of both possession and physical disease.

Christ also empowered the Apostles and disciples to cast out demons in His name while He Himself was still on earth (Mt 10:1, 8; Mk 6:7; Lk 9:1, 10:17), and to believers in general He promised the same power (Mk 16:17). But this delegated power was conditional, for the Apostles were not always successful in their exorcisms: Some types of spirits could only be cast out by prayer and fasting (Mt 17:15, 20; Mk 9:27-28; Lk 9:40).

Yet in the end, success was promised for those who believed in the power and authority of God (Mk 16:17; Acts 16:18, 19:12). This same power and authority was used within the Apostolic Church and continued down through the ages, uninterrupted to the present day. In our modern world of knowledge and technological achievement, is
it really possible that true cases of diabolical possession occur?

According to Ed Warren, American demonologist, well over six hundred major exorcisms have been performed between 1970 and 1980 in North America alone (The Demonologist).

Private Exorcism

A **private exorcism** is an informal act that consists of a command given in the name of Jesus to any evil spirit to leave an afflicted or oppressed person. The very word private is significant, for it means that there is no liturgical rite or particular formula to follow, and that the minister is acting in his or her own name, not that of the Church. Furthermore, a private exorcism is not commissioned by ecclesiastical authorities, nor is the minister given a specific and official delegation or mission from the Church to perform such an act.

A private exorcism is used in cases of temptation and oppression, never with diabolical possession, which is authorized by the bishop or his delegate. It may be performed at any time one has a reason to believe that another person is being afflicted by an evil spirit.

Any person may perform a **simple exorcism**: both men and women of the laity, as well as deacons, nuns, and priests. Indeed, throughout Church history, dogmatic theologians have claimed that private exorcism is the ministerial duty of all the faithful, and can be prayed without special permission of the bishop.

Yet it must be acknowledged that a priest usually has greater authority over an evil spirit than a layperson by virtue of his special grace and authorized ministry on behalf of the Church. It must also be acknowledged that a certain **charism for exorcism** does exist. This charism may or may not be found in a particular priest; likewise, it may be found equally in a gifted layperson.

The private exorcism is really a command to the evil spirit in Jesus' name. Preceding the exorcism, it is wise for the minister to pray for protection from the evil spirit. A prayer to the Holy Spirit is made for grace to be given to the one who is being prayed for so that he or she may overcome the forces of evil. After the demon has left, a prayer of thanksgiving is recommended.

The prayer of exorcism should be said quietly, without spoken words, whenever possible. If the victim does not know the prayer is being said, it may be for the better. When one explains to a victim that he or she may be under the influence or attack of an evil spirit, it can often cause panic, depression, paranoia, or extreme emotional distress.

When the victim senses a diabolical problem and voluntarily asks for a deliverance prayer, the spoken word may be appropriate. If this is not the case, or if someone else requests the prayer on behalf of another person, then a simple silent prayer may be in order.

Before a private exorcism takes place, it is recommended that the victim make a true confession and be absolved of any sins for which he remains in guilt. This practice has been encouraged in the Church since the time of St. Alphonsus Liguori (1696-1787) down to modern times (witness today's manuals of moral theology).

There are really two categories of exorcisms: minor and major. A **minor exorcism** takes the form of a blessing. Although unknown to most people, this is a basic rite of exorcism. Baptism is actually an **exorcism ritual**, and it is probably one reason why few people ever fall victim to diabolical oppression or possession. Minor exorcisms may clear a house of evil spirits or rid a person of negative spirits that may bring about subtle attacks. Major exorcisms are proper to **solemn or formal exorcisms** authorized by
the ecclesiastical members of the Church.

Deliverance Prayer

Deliverance ministry involving simple prayers offered by the laity for protection against evil spirits was recognized and practiced in the very early Church. As early as A.D. 150, St. Justin Martyr declared in his Dialogue With Trypho that every evil spirit exorcised in the name of Jesus Christ was overcome and expelled.

In the third century, the Apostolic Tradition of Hippolytus claims that baptismal candidates were allowed to go through exorcisms by their godparents, by their teacher at the end of each weekly instruction, and before baptism by the bishop (Proof of the Apostolic Preaching).

Even today, the period of the catechumenate involves minor exorcisms. Although the laity frequently performed minor exorcisms (deliverance prayers) during the first few centuries of the Church, in time the practice was reserved by the saints or the priests.

Modern-day deliverance ministry originally stems from the 1967 Catholic renewal movement in the United States, which soon included the charismatic movement. These original renewal groups were highly influenced by the fundamentalist, Pentecostal, or Free Churches of the Protestant denomination. It was from these sources that the
early Catholic movement got its inspiration, for the Protestant groups published many books and articles related to this ministry that were lacking in Catholic publishing houses.

Borrowing from these works, the early Catholic renewal groups were inspired with the fundamentalist approach of the devil and his demons. Thus, the fire and brimstone sermons of the Protestant Pentecostals were incorporated into the views of many of these early Catholic followers.

Catholic deliverance ministry as we know it today evolved from these fundamentalist denominations. These groups stress the role of the small group or individual, as well as biblical literalism and fundamentalism to gain victory over the powers of darkness. Cooperation and involvement with ecclesiastical figures of the Church bishops, priests, deacons seem to be strangely absent from most of these sessions.

Of course, the danger with such an approach is that Catholic deliverance groups assume a theology that is not very Catholic at all; rather, they cling more closely to various Protestant Pentecostal churches from which they originally developed. This is not true for all deliverance groups, but it occurs with such frequency that caution must be exercised when investigating their ministry.

Perhaps that is why some ecclesiastical authorities in the Church have been slow to accept such a widespread deliverance ministry made up of predominantly lay people. A serious question arises at this point: Where does the ministry of a simple deliverance prayer end and the formal or solemn exorcism reserved for the Church begin?

A clear distinction must be made concerning the legitimate ministry of deliverance. Diabolical possession (**total bondage**) requires a solemn exorcism authorized by the local bishop or his delegate; diabolical oppression (partial bondage) needs only deliverance prayer. Possession involves the internal takeover of a body by an evil spirit, whereas with oppression the demon influences or afflicts a victim from outside the body.

Another danger brought on by the ministry of deliverance involves an excessive preoccupation with demonic spirits. The rise in demonism has evolved because of the increase in media products that emphasize the devil (movies and books) as well as the occult practices. It is no mere coincidence that the dramatic increase in deliverance ministry is a result of such saturation of the public interest.

The Church has always exercised great caution when investigating claims of diabolical intervention, consulting with scientific and medical experts before an alleged case may be considered authentic. Only after all natural causes have been considered does the Church admit to the possibility of a diabolical oppression or possession.

Thus, an authentication of a true case of diabolical possession is rare, as is an authorized solemn exorcism. Since the Church rarely authorizes a formal exorcism, it may be that the smaller, private deliverance groups have increased across the country to fill the void left by the discretion of the Church. In other words, like the example of water, the public curiosity and fascination with demonic influence may seek its own level, so to speak.

Many who are involved with the deliverance ministry deny that they are practicing any type of exorcism. Knowing that a formal exorcism must be approved by the local bishop or his delegate, many who practice deliverance attempt to describe their ministry in such a way so as not to appear like they are trespassing on forbidden ground; thus, they label their ministry with more neutral connotations: They speak of `deliverance' sessions, `liberation,' `prayer of welcome,' `special prayer,' `prayer of compassion,' `intercessory prayer,' etc. (Renewal and the Powers of Darkness: Malines Document IV).

According to Cardinal Suenens, there are various reasons why those who practice deliverance use such watered-down language: (1) they may be afraid of scaring away the people they wish to help; (2) they might want to avoid a confrontation with ecclesiastical authorities, who may suspect that deliverance sessions are nothing more than unauthorized contraband exorcisms; or (3) they may wish to keep their activities from generating unhealthy curiosity or unbalanced enthusiasm.

Typically, a deliverance session involves several stages of activity.

The first is known as a preparatory stage, where the deliverance group offers various prayers and asks God for guidance and discernment.

The second phase is that of the **prayer of deliverance**, which includes the following: the beginning prayer of praise and petition; a prayer to bind the evil spirit in order that all who are present may be protected; a series of questions designed to discover the names and functions of the evil spirits who are responsible for the affliction, thereby enabling the group to better prepare for the deliverance; and a prayer of the victim, who is encouraged to renounce the sins that caused the affliction.

In the final phase, prayers of thanksgiving are offered by everyone present. Then the deliverance team decides upon the necessary follow-up meetings involving further prayers, as well as possible counseling and support for the former victim of the diabolical affliction.

During the deliverance sessions, various techniques and objects may be used. For some, a crucifix, blessed salt, or holy water is used. Many groups prefer to look into the eyes of the afflicted victim during the entire time of the deliverance session; others believe in keeping their eyes closed and instead concentrate on the intercessory role of the Holy Spirit.

In many sessions, loud voices are used to identify and expel the presence of the demon. Others prefer to use a silent, gentle voice in their ministry, since it is God's power that will overcome and not their own gestures or actions.

Excessive theatrical displays have often been witnessed at such deliverance sessions. This has always been common with Protestant Pentecostal groups, and many Catholic charismatics also employ excessive emotional displays (Robert Faricy, S.J., quoted in Deliverance Prayer by Fathers Dennis and Matthew Linn, S.J.). Deliverance sessions can range from one meeting to several months' sessions, depending upon the seriousness of the affliction and the success of the support group.

The questions posed by the practitioners to the demon who allegedly oppresses or possesses the victim are designed to identify the evil spirit and its activities: Who are you? How many are you? How long have you dwelled in him? Where exactly do you dwell in him? What illness have you caused him? Then a command in the name of Jesus Christ is used to expel the demon from the helpless victim. Obviously, these actions are based upon the teachings of Scripture and are often used during a formal exorcism. Yet the issue is not whether these acts are legitimate tactics against the powers of darkness. Rather, how do these deliverance groups know that a demon is behind the problem to begin with? Are there experts among the group (physicians, psychologists, psychiatrists, theologians, etc.) who are discerning the affliction from a scientific or medical viewpoint? Are all members of the deliverance group truly gifted with discernment? Do the practitioners have any former hands-on experience with a formal exorcism? How long of a training period do the members need to be qualified exorcists or demonologists?

The Church usually only assigns **diocesan exorcists** who have proven their knowledge, faith, and moral character through many years of service.) Is the victim an impressionable person who sees a demon in his or her mind when none is actually there? Does the victim's feelings influence the general consensus of the deliverance practitioners, even if he or she is wrong? (Mass hypnosis and suggestion have influenced common opinions in various life situations.)

Again, where does the simple prayer of deliverance end and the act of exorcism begin? If these groups are identifying evil spirits and demanding they leave in the name of Jesus, are they delving into areas reserved for the ecclesiastical authority of the Church? Many questions such as these need to be answered when dealing with the
ministry of deliverance.

Solemn Exorcism

According to H. Noldin in Summa Theologia Moralis, a solemn exorcism is the formal act of expelling an evil spirit or evil spirits from the body of a person. This solemn act is also known as a formal or public exorcism: formal because it is done through a series of elaborate instructions set down in the Roman Ritual, and public because it is done in the name of and with the authority of the Church.

Noldin goes on to make the following distinctions of exorcisms: (1) **solemn exorcism**, which is for the purpose of driving out the devil; **simple exorcism**, which is for the purpose of curbing the devil's power lest he harm people or things; (3) **public exorcism**, which involves ministers of the Church who expel the demon in the name and with the authority of the Church; and (4) **private exorcism**, when the exorcist acts in his own name.

Moreover, in Noldin's view, the difference between a solemn and simple exorcism is one based upon pastoral needs. A solemn exorcism is needed if a person is possessed; a simple exorcism is needed for curbing the power of the devil. On the other hand, the distinction between public and private exorcisms is also well-defined. A public exorcism requires the authority of the Church; private exorcisms only involve a person who acts in his own name as a Christian to rid the evil presence.

Solemn exorcisms, as pointed out in the fourth volume of Opera Omnia, should only be used in cases of authentic diabolical possession. Solemn exorcisms are restricted to those who have both the power of authority and the power of jurisdiction. The power of order is needed because a formal exorcism pertains to an act of the ecclesiastical order and can only be performed by a consecrated minister.

.

The power of jurisdiction is required because Canon 1151 in the previous Code of Canon Law (code 1172 in the new Code) states that only a priest specifically chosen and approved by the local bishop can perform a public exorcism. In turn, this canon law dates back to Pope Innocent I (401-417), and was reaffirmed at the Synod of Naples (see the first of volume of Acta et Decreta).

Why does the Church limit solemn exorcisms to priests? According to one belief, as expounded in Theologia Moralis by such experts as Sabetto-Barretti and Scanini, it is done in order to take precautions against abuses and also because the law applies to exempt religious in their own churches in case abuses arise.

What is an **authentic possession**? It is where a demon enters a person's body, takes up residence there, dominates the personality, and frustrates the person's exercise of free will.

A lengthy Church tradition supports the reality of demonic possession. St. Alphonsus Liguori (1696-1787), Doctor of the Church, once claimed that possessions are real and should not be mistaken for fantasies or corporeal temptations (Praxis Confessarii). Furthermore, Alphonsus states that even when a diabolical temptation has occurred, a confessor should pronounce a simple exorcism against the demon in this way: I, as a minister of God, command you, unclean spirit, to depart from this creature of God.

In 1860, the Council of Prague stated that the devil not only can possess but can also cause diseases in men. It is the Church's weapon against the demon to perform the solemn act of exorcism. Shortly after, in 1865, the Council of Vienna declared that although diabolical possession does occur, it is a rare phenomenon.

The great spiritual theologian Tanquerey talked about possession and exorcism in a chapter called Extraordinary Mystical Phenomena in his famous work The Spiritual Life.

The Confrontation

Processes of Possession

A general outline of the process of possession as described in Hostage to the Devil may be thought of in these terms: (1) the entry point; (2) erroneous judgments; and (3) the voluntary yielding of control.

During the **entry point**, the evil spirit enters an individual and a decision is made by the victim to allow that entry. As we have seen, this entry point coincides with the open-door theory: A victim must willingly and consciously give permission for the demon to intrude upon his or her life. This can occur through dabbling with the occult, personality malfunctions, repetitive and unconfessed sin, curses, pacts with the devil, and so on. At least a part of human will must be freely given in order for the evil spirit to enter the victim's life.

During the stage of erroneous judgments, the possessed weakens during vital moments that determine whether or not he or she will succumb to evil and ignore the grace of God. Here is where one makes a series of personal judgments that will affect his character and prepare him for the critical stage of yielding control to the demon. During this period of judgment, the victim may find that his original strength, beauty, and idealism are slowly, piece by piece, turned upside down.

The voluntary yielding of control is the actual decisive moment when the human will chooses for or against evil. If this will is abandoned to the evil spirit, then the victim is in danger of being taken over by the invading force. At first, this intrusion amounts to diabolical oppression. If allowed to continue, the victim may become **partially possessed (demonic bondage)**. In time, if the entire will is dominated by the demon, a perfect or complete possession may result. Although this final step is rare, it does occur from time to time. It is during this final phase when the evil spirit is able to invade the victim from within, taking over his entire personality and thought processes.

The following patterns that emerge during a solemn exorcism were suggested by the former Jesuit professor at the Pontifical Biblical Institute in Rome, Malachi Martin. Although the author has inserted his own comments throughout these stages, the terms and succession of events is recorded in Mr. Martin's book Hostage to the Devil.

The Presence

During the early stages of a formal exorcism, a strong and undeniable sense of evil is perceived by all who are present.

Although the demon attempts to hide or masquerade his presence, this feeling is too strong to remain unnoticed. It is not any particular phenomenon that one can touch, taste, feel, or see; rather, the demon exposes itself through an eerie sense that what is present is totally inhuman and immoral.

This **inhumanness** is not felt in a particular spot or location. Instead, the overwhelming presence of evil is detected all around those in attendance: above, below, behind, and in front. Although one cannot verbalize his or her knowledge of this presence, nevertheless it is known to the instinct and the spirit.

Since pure evil is spirit, the fact that the demon is totally inhuman reaches to the very depths of one's soul. It also touches the very fabric of one's will. Never before and never again will one feel this total conflict of good versus evil. Suddenly, there is the painful reality that one's face-to-face with the very essence of all that is opposed to the sacredness of human life. A suffocating feeling of hatred fills the room. One is more alone than at any other point in his life. Fear and panic clutch the soul; confusion may linger in the mind. At times, a hiss in the brain causes great discomfort.

Above all, a frightening sense of doom fills the air. One recognizes somehow that this inhuman presence is not to be taken lightly. In fact, there is an overwhelming feeling that this presence is both powerful and dangerous. It is the unseen that sees, the unknown that knows all. And no wonder the feeling of fear prevails: One is now in the presence of a personal being more intelligent than any human ever created, one who knows infinitely more than anyone in history.

After all, this presence has been around since the beginning of creation. It is able to read the deepest secrets of all who are near, even the smallest and darkest of sins.

For those involved with the demonic enemy, it is painfully clear that he exposes those past sins during the course of the confrontation. No one is immune from his attacks, no sin is too small to go unnoticed (especially those that have not been confessed).

The early attack is not only psychological but very powerful and effective. Only the well-prepared can face the evil one: those who have fasted and prayed; those who have a clear conscience; the physically fit; and those who remain steadfast and firm in their faith in Christ. Without these characteristics, one is bound to fall to the snares of the enemy.

The Pretense

During the early phase of the exorcism, the priest must force the evil spirit to make itself known. As was indicated before, the invading spirit attempts to hide behind its victim. This masquerade is called the **pretense**.

Knowing that an exorcism is most painful, the diabolical being resists all efforts to identify himself. The demon is most effective when he does his dirty work unnoticed, when his victims fall unchecked. This is the frightening thing about the evil spirit: the crafty and subtle way he lures his victims. Many victims have fallen without the slightest clue as to the source of their downfall. Sometimes the takeover is a gradual process that extends over many years; at other times, the attack is quick and violent.

During the pretense, all assistants to the exorcist are at risk of both physical and psychological attack. Yet of all who are present, it is the exorcising priest who is the real target. The exorcist is acutely aware that his very life is on the line. Once provoked, the evil spirit will soon answer with an all-out attack. The priest must be strong and determined, for the evil spirit will attempt to break down his confidence and destroy his very will. It is a meeting of the minds, a clash between pure good and evil.

Once the exorcist has challenged the evil spirit to battle, there is no turning back. If he does, he will become a target of diabolical assault for the remainder of his life. If he goes on but loses the battle, he could be killed. Worse yet, the evil spirit will attempt to take over the mind and will of the exorcist.

If the demon succeeds, the priest may lose more than his earthly life he could in fact lose his eternal soul. This is no contest for amateurs. In fact, there are really no experts against this mystery of iniquity that has thought and acted long before the creation of humanity. Only one's faith in Christ and only through the actual power of Christ will the exorcist ever hope to succeed. Left alone to his own recourse, the exorcist takes on a dangerous mission that he alone cannot win. The demon is simply too powerful, too knowledgeable, and too strong. Even Jesus had difficulty with the evil spirits. Only the foolish would attempt to conquer pure evil on his own good terms.

The Breakpoint

If the exorcist remains firm through the end of the pretense, he suddenly encounters stronger psychological attacks from the invading spirit. Now he becomes a direct target of diabolical assault, aimed at destroying his will.

The evil spirit will use a variety of tactics to confuse and frighten the exorcising priest. Contradictions of every kind go through the mind of the exorcist, causing him to momentarily falter. Suddenly, the priest may experience different phenomena through his physical senses: Putrid smells may be sensed through the ears; loud, screeching noises appear to be heard through his eyes; foul tastes seem to come from his nose; etc. Agonizing pressure may be felt inside his head to the point where it feels like it will explode. Tremendous headaches may be experienced, accompanied by loud, buzzing sounds that pierce the brain. Clearly, the evil spirit is warning the exorcist of impending danger.

The Voice

After the moment of breakpoint, the demonic spirit reveals his identity through a variety of frightening sounds. At first, the words may come slowly from the victim's mouth. Then one becomes aware that what is being heard is alien. The sounds may manifest themselves as growls, babblings, laughter, hissing, sneering, etc. It is not unusual to hear animal sounds or screams. The voice first manifests itself in order to frustrate the process of the exorcism. If the exorcism is to be successful, the priest must silence the voice. This is normally done through the name and authority of Jesus Christ.

The Clash

When the voice has been successfully silenced, a tremendous pressure may be felt inside the exorcist. This pressure may be a steady hissing in the brain, or a dreadful uneasy feeling in the depths of one's soul.

At this point, **the clash** has arrived. This is a phase whereby the evil spirit and the exorcist confront each other for the victory of the will. Never before will the exorcist seem so totally alone. Now the evil spirit will attempt to break the exorcist's concentration and frustrate him into despair. Only through the power and grace of Christ can the exorcist hope to win the battle. If the priest gives in at this stage, he will lose the battle to the evil spirit. Worst yet, the devil is after his very soul. Be that as it may, the exorcist must persevere and attempt to expel the demon.

Expulsion

Expulsion of the evil spirit usually comes after the exorcist has successfully forced the spirit to identify himself. In some strange way, identification appears to make the demon vulnerable: He is now exposed, whereas before he worked most effectively through anonymity and deception.

Because the evil spirit knows nothing but lies (Jn 8:44), identification forces the demon to deal with the truth, even if only for a moment. It is then that the faith and perseverance of the exorcist will gain the advantage; the power of Christ will work through the exorcist and force the possessing spirit to depart in His name.

When the exorcism is successful, everyone in the room will notice an immediate absence of the presence. All feelings of fear and suffocation disappear. The victim of the possession, once tormented and changed, now appears to be his or her normal self. Absent are the inhuman sounds and voices, gone are the physiological changes that plagued the victim during the possession. An indescribable feeling of joy and relief fill the hearts of all who are present at the site.

After the expulsion, the former victim must be encouraged to pray regularly, receive the sacraments, and go to confession frequently. A false sense of confidence may develop in the one who had been possessed. Yet he or she must be warned that if the same circumstances are presented again, the demon may return, bringing back more possessing demons. Then the victim will be in greater danger than before, and another exorcism will prove to be much more difficult to achieve: When the unclean spirit has gone out of a man, he passes through waterless places seeking rest; and finding none he says, `I will return to my house from which I came.' And when he comes he finds it swept and put in order. Then he goes and brings seven other spirits more evil than himself, and they enter and dwell there; and the last state of that man becomes worse than the first (Lk 11:24-26).

Many situations, conditions, or practices may have caused the demon to intrude to begin with: dabbling with the occult (Ouija board, seances, tarot cards, etc.); alcohol or drugs; sexually immoral acts; Satanism or witchcraft; depression; suicide attempts; murder; and so on. If the demon returns and repossesses the individual, physical death is likely to occur. It is also possible that there would be no second chance for grace: The demon may successfully win the soul of the victim for all eternity.

The Exorcist

Background

An **exorcist** is anyone who exorcises or professes to exorcise demons in the name of Jesus Christ (Acts 19:13). It used to be one who was ordained by the local bishop for this office, the second of the four minor orders of the Western Church. The practice of exorcism was not confined to clerics in the early ages, as is clear from Tertullian (Pologt; see De Idolat.) and Origen (Celsum). Indeed, Origen has stated that even the simplest and rudest of the faithful sometimes cast out demons, by a mere prayer or adjuration (see Mk 15:17).

In the Eastern Church, a specially ordained order of exorcists (or of acolytes, or doorkeepers) has never been established, but in the Western Church, these three minor orders (with that of lectors as a fourth) were instituted shortly before the middle of the third century.

Pope Cornelius (251-253) mentions in his letter to Fabius that there were then in the Roman Catholic Church forty-two acolytes, and fifty-two exorcists, readers, and doorkeepers (Ecclesiastical History), and the institution of these orders as well as the organization of their functions seems to have been the work of Cornelius's predecessor, Pope Fabian (236-250).

The fourth Council of Carthage (398), in its seventh canon, prescribes the **rite of ordination** for exorcist. The bishop gives the candidate a book that contains the **formula for exorcism**. Then he says, Receive, and commit to memory, and possess the power of imposing hands on energumens, whether baptized or catechumens.

This basic rite had gone unchanged until the seventeenth century. In earlier times, one of the chief duties of the exorcist was to take part in baptismal exorcism. Catechumens were exorcised frequently, often before the actual baptismal rite. After the institution of the order of exorcist, exorcism was still forbidden to the laity; nor did those who exorcised, according to Exorcism Through the Ages, always use the forms contained in the Book of Exorcisms.

Qualities

The Apostolic Constitutions (VIII, 26; P.G., I, 1122) says that the exorcist is not ordained for the special **office of exorcist**, but that if anyone possess the charismatic power, he is to be recognized, and if need be, ordained deacon or subdeacon. This practice has survived in the Eastern Orthodox Church.

In Christian countries authentic cases of possession sometimes occur and every priest, especially if he is a parish priest, or pastor, is liable to be called upon to perform his duty as exorcist. If this be the case, he must abide by the rules set down in the Ritual, which requires that the local bishop be consulted, and his authorization obtained before exorcism is attempted.

A case of possession should never be taken for granted. The priest who undertakes the office should himself be humble. He should also prepare himself for the work by special acts of devotion and mortification, particularly by prayer and fasting (Mt 17:20). The exorcist should avoid in the course of the rite everything that savors of superstition, and should leave the medical aspects of the case to qualified physicians.

The priest should admonish the possessed, insofar as the victim is capable, to dispose himself for the exorcism by prayer, fasting, confession, and Holy Communion, and while the rite is in progress to excite within himself a lively faith in God's goodness, and a patient resignation to His holy will (Exorcism Through the Ages).

The exorcist is usually an older man, between the ages of forty and eighty. He tends to be a very saintly, humble man who cares deeply about people and their welfare. Usually he has no title other than monk, priest, rabbi, or minister, but he seems to embody a combination of wisdom, kindness, and compassion that one doesn't see in ordinary people (The Demonologist).

Yet, as Ed Warren claims in The Demonologist, piety, wisdom, devotion, and humility are not enough. As a person, the exorcist must embody the virtues of goodness and morality that represent the very best aspects of man. And no less important, the exorcist must be strong enough to withstand the mental and physical torments that frequently occur in the struggle to win back a human soul from the clutches of the devil. At some time in his life, without exception, the demon attacks the exorcist for being the good man that he is.

The exorcist's task is the most thankless job on earth. Although he may be a man of enormous personal stature, he is often chastised and ridiculed by those too ignorant to recognize his worth.

The exorcist normally has a background in parish ministry. Rarely is he the scholarly type, nor is he usually a recently ordained priest. Good physical health is not a requirement for an exorcist, nor is an intellectual brilliance, postgraduate degree, or a sophisticated cultural background. Rather, the exorcist must have exceptional qualities of moral judgment, personal behavior, and religious belief.

Procedures

In earlier days, one priest was chosen as the diocesan exorcist in every diocese throughout the Catholic Church. This is no longer the case because of the dramatic drop in reported incidents involving authentic diabolical oppression and possession.

In the modern era, there is still one priest in every diocese who might be called upon to perform a solemn exorcism, but his assignment is not formally or publicly announced. Rather, the diocesan bishop will usually assign a respected priest the role of exorcist privately in case his services are ever needed. Why is this so?

One reason is that the Catholic Church has come under great scrutiny and criticism over the years about her teachings and activities concerning the diabolical world: temptation, oppression, possession, exorcism, and so on. The era of the Inquisition and the witch trials didn't help the Church's credibility either, for those were times when the devil was seen behind every bush and every action. It was a time of excessive preoccupation with the **preternatural world**.

Added to the fact that medicine and science have eliminated many alleged cases of demonic possession with verifiable natural causes, the Church is obviously more discreet and prudent about her willingness to identify a diabolical experience as an authentic case of oppression or possession.

This is not to say that she has changed her teachings on demonology one bit. With the wisdom of the ages, the Church has rightfully come to a certain maturity through the years. This maturity involves careful investigation, introspection, spiritual discernment, and prudent judgment on all levels concerned.

Thus, when the Church does admit to an authentic case of demonic possession, she has taken great care in being extremely critical and thorough in order to rule out all possibility of natural causes for such a phenomenon. After all, the wisdom and authority of the Church are at stake in a world that looks to criticize everything under the sun, anyway. Some may be frustrated by the seemingly skeptical attitude of ecclesiastical members of the faith. This may be so, but it is necessary all the same.

When a major exorcism is conducted, the date, time, and location of the ritual is usually fixed beforehand, whenever possible. Preference is given to holy days or the feast days of saints. The ritual is normally scheduled for the morning hours to avoid the assaults of the devil, who as the Prince of Darkness is capable of launching devastating assaults during the hours of night.

Before the exorcism occurs, the exorcist prepares himself by fasting and taking blessed water only when necessary. This is known as the **black fast**. Spiritually, the exorcist will cloister himself in prayer for a minimum of three days in order to be emboldened with the three theological virtues of faith, hope, and love: faith in what he is doing; hope that he will be successful; and love in giving himself freely in the interest of another. Finally, having put himself in a state of grace, the exorcist will implore divine assistance, because no man has the power within himself to fight these **powers of darkness**.

It is recommended that the exorcism take place in a church or some sacred place. But if this is not possible because of sickness or some other legitimate reason, it should occur in a private house. There is usually a sense of urgency to get on with the exorcism as soon as possible, lest the victim suffer further pain or anguish. There is another reason for acting quickly: The victim may be only suffering from diabolical oppression or partial possession.

Furthermore, if a possession is partial, the exorcist does not want to delay any further to give the demon a chance to succeed at perfect (complete) possession.

On the day of the exorcism, assistants who have prepared themselves for the ritual by prayer and fasting will assemble.

One of the assistants is usually a young priest appointed by diocesan authorities who will train for the role of future diocesan exorcist. This assistant priest will help to monitor the exorcist's words and actions, warn him if he is making a mistake, help him if he weakens physically, and replace him if he dies, collapses, flees, or is physically or emotionally battered beyond endurance during the course of the exorcism.

The lay assistants are usually chosen by the exorcist, as is the time of the exorcism. The lay assistants are usually large, healthy men, whose strength might be needed to restrain the possessed victim if he or she becomes violent, levitates off the bed, or attempts to desecrate religious items in the room. Among the lay assistants will be a medical doctor in case anyone present at the exorcism suffers from shock, emotional strain, or physical injury.

Four is the normal number of lay assistants present, although at times there may be no one available to help the exorcist (this has been the case in remote areas where there are few people around).

If the potential for violence is evident during the exorcism, the possessed will be laid out on a bed in loose-fitting clothing. Anything that can move, burn, or be thrown must be removed from the room: Carpets, rugs, pictures, curtains, tables, stands, chairs, boxes, trunks, bedclothes, bureaus, chandeliers all must go. The only thing necessary in the room is a table where candles, holy oils, and the Blessed Sacrament are placed. All furniture and objects will have to be taken away to help assure the safety of all who are present. Windows are usually nailed or boarded over to prevent the demon from throwing people or objects out of it.

Because of the fact that dresser drawers often bang and shut uncontrollably during the exorcism, they will need to be fastened, locked, or nailed shut as well. Doors present a peculiar problem. They, too, are subject to opening and shutting in a violent banging manner. Yet the exorcists or his assistants may need to leave the room from time to time in lengthy exorcisms, so securing the door is not always possible. It is recommended that the door remain closed during the rite and that the space under the door be covered. Because the demonic force is so powerful, the vicinity immediately outside the room of the exorcism must be protected lest the diabolical force affect others outside the hostile environment.

All idle and curious questioning of the demon ought to be avoided, and the prayers need to be read with great faith, humility, and fervor, done in a spirit of power and authority. The Blessed Sacrament is not to be brought too close to the possessed because of the possibility of irreverence. But the crucifix, holy water, and, when available, relics of the saints are to be employed. If expulsion of the evil spirit does not occur the first time around, the rite should be repeated, if need be, several times.

Once begun, there are no timeouts, except to allow for the few necessities that must be taken into account: going to the bathroom, taking some food, getting a brief breath of fresh air outside the room, and the like.

The only people who dress in a special way during the exorcism are the exorcist and his **priest-assistant**. Each will wear a long black cassock that covers him from neck to feet. Over the cassock will be a purple stole, which is worn around the neck and hangs loosely the length of the torso.

There are a few cardinal rules that are determined for most exorcisms. The priest in charge must insist on the following before the exorcism begins: (1) everyone present is to obey each and every command the exorcist makes without question or delay; (2) no one can take the initiative for any words or actions without the express permission of the exorcist; and (3) no one is allowed to ever speak to the possessed person for any reason at any time.

Furthermore, the exorcist must prepare each of the assistants beforehand about the possible experiences they might encounter: obscene or vulgar behavior; foul language; potential for blood, excrement, or vomit at the site; personal insults aimed at each individual; secrets or sins disclosed by the demon that might embarrass anyone in the room; foul smells or odors; sacrilegious actions; loud noises; disorientation; etc.

Investigative Procedures

Signs of Possession

Although reports and recommendations submitted by medical examiners and the officiating demonologist may often be enough to convince Church authorities of the need for exorcism, usually additional evidence must be brought forth to further prove that an authentic possession has taken place: Tape recordings, photographs, test-instrument readings, or materialized substances and objects are often submitted as hard physical evidence that such a phenomenon has indeed occurred. In addition, eyewitness testimony is sought under strict guidelines and procedures.

A series of specific questions must be answered before the Church allows a formal exorcism: (1) Has the individual divulged hidden or future knowledge? (2) Has the possessed individual spoken in tongues or languages unknown to him? (3) Has the individual demonstrated inhuman powers, or brought about activity distinctly beyond the bounds of human ability? (4) Has the possessing entity identified itself by name or given some indisputable sign of a diabolical presence? These questions must be answered according to the procedures found in the Roman Ritual.

Demonologist Ed Warren has claimed that in six out of ten cases of exorcism, the spirit obeys the commands of the exorcist and leaves on the first reading of the ritual. But in four out of ten cases, there is trouble (The Demonologist).

Phenomena occur in the room, and the possessing spirits put up a strong resistance. The evil spirits rely upon **counter assaults** in an attempt to stop the exorcism from continuing. Screams may be heard, or hootings will come from the person who is possessed. Other noises experienced are: howlings, whinnying of horses, barking of dogs, snorting of pigs, and similar animal sounds.

Vulgar language may come from the mouth of the possessed: blasphemies, foul words, gutter talk, etc.

At times, the evil spirit will challenge the Scriptures being read, especially if the exorcist makes the slightest error in fact or pronunciation. The insults and slanderings are intended to demoralize all who are involved with the exorcism.

As the exorcism advances, more frightening or repulsive phenomena may occur through the possessing spirit: The possessed may levitate off the bed; psychic burns and slashes may cover the victim's body; gallons of putrid, disgusting substances may be vomited from the possessed victim's mouth; the torso may become bloated to twice its normal size, and the skin may appear to be cracking open because of the phenomena; excrement may spontaneously appear on the floor, or the victim may urinate copiously during the ritual; foul and unbearable odors of urine or sulphur may suddenly appear in the room; freezing temperatures or hot spots may suddenly appear and last throughout the exorcism; bodily levitation may be experienced by the one who is possessed; etc.

Objects such as crucifixes may explode spontaneously in the home. Glass items are especially vulnerable, which makes those present in particular danger. It is not an uncommon experience for many to claim that they were cut severely by glass objects that were hurled at them at high speeds, causing the items to shatter on their arms, chest, or head. Chairs, kitchen utensils, knives, or items on any shelf are liable to be thrown at those who are present in the room. Thus, it is imperative that all loose or moveable objects be taken from the room before the exorcism commences.

Strange welts may appear on the skin of the possessed victim. Oftentimes, these welts will form a message of help from the victim. Please help me! or Pray for me! are common phrases that appear out of the skin. In some cases, the welts become festered and emit pus as a result of the cracking of the skin. A few witnesses have reported seeing the muscles literally protrude out of these cracks, looking as if the victim is going to explode.

In instances where fluids appear spontaneously or are ejected from the victim's mouth, it has been reported that literally gallons of the substance may issue forth at the scene. The fluids have been described in various fashions: as a combination of spaghetti and hair; excrement; pools of odorous urine; a white, sticky substance; bloody vomit; and other nauseating things.

A common sign that occurs during authentic demonic intrusions is that of hair pulling. With vengeance, an unseen force may rip out sections of hair from the scalp of the victim. In other instances, the victim's arm is pulled or the victim is choked. Punches have been reported in various possession cases, whereby the victim is noticeably bruised by the blows of the unseen force. Black eyes, swollen limbs, and even broken arms have been witnessed.

In the truly possessed person, the reflexes appear to be sporadic or abnormal, sometimes disappearing for a time. Breathing may appear to stop for long periods. The heartbeat is hard to detect, and the face may be distorted, sometimes abnormally tight and at other times so smooth that there appears to be no line or wrinkle anywhere on the skin.

A phenomenon known as **possessed gravity** has been observed. When this happens, the possessed becomes physically immovable, or those who surround him are so weighed down by an unseen suffocating force that everyone is helplessly bound.

A vital test is always conducted for the verification of authentic diabolical oppression or possession: It is known as religious provocation. This is a means whereby the evil spirit is challenged to reveal or identify himself in a particular location or within a specific person. This challenge is designed to anger the evil spirit or to frighten him into submission. Needless to say, **religious provocation** is extremely dangerous and should not be performed by anyone who has no experience with such matters. Usually, a parish priest or a trained demonologist initiates the provocation.

Provocation occurs mainly through three types of actions: (1) readings of Sacred Scripture; (2) prayers recited in the presence of the unclean spirit; and (3) explosion of a blessed object such as a relic or a cross. If an evil spirit is present, he normally will manifest himself under religious provocation. This **manifestation** comes in the form of physical or psychological attack, poltergeist activity, or through voices that appear to come out of nowhere. These attacks are dangerous, often causing serious harm to the provoker.

At first, the demon issues warning signs to the one who wishes to expose or expel him. Some of the warnings include threatening voices aimed at frightening the one who confronts the spirit; objects thrown at the provoker but intentionally missing him; suffocating or foul odors in the air; and vulgar or blasphemous writings that appear spontaneously on the wall. The evil spirit wants it to be clearly known that this is not a game to be taken lightly. If pressed, the diabolic being will make a full-scaled attempt to harm the person or frighten him away. Yet the provocation must be done in order to force the demon out of his obscurity and into the open. Only then will the challenge through the rite of solemn exorcism successfully rid the place or person of the evil spirit.

Vincentius von Berg, in his Enchiridium (Cologne, 1743), gave the following signs to look for in cases of authentic diabolical possession:

1. They [the possessed] often desire the worst food.

2. They are unable to retain their food, are irked by continual vomiting, and are unable to digest.

3. Others experience a heavy weight in the stomach, as if a sort of ball ascended from the stomach into the gullet, which they seem to vomit forth, yet nevertheless it returns to its original position.

4. Some feel a gnawing in the lower belly; others feel either a rapid pulsation in the neck or pain in the kidneys. Others feel a

continuous pain in the head or brain, beyond endurance, on account of which they seem oppressed, shattered, or pierced.

5. They may have trouble with their heart, which feels as if torn by dogs, or eaten by serpents, or pierced by nails and needles, or constricted and stifled.

6. At other times, all parts of their head swell up, so that throughout their body they feel such lassitude that they can scarcely move.

7.Some experience frequent and sudden pains, which they cannot describe, but they shriek aloud.

8. In others, the body is weakened and reduced to a shadow on account of extraordinary emaciation, impotency or vigor, and extreme languor.

9. At other times, their limbs feel whipped, torn, bound, or constricted, especially the heart and bones.

10. Some are accustomed to feel something like the coldest wind or a fiery flame run through their stomach, causing the most violent contractions in their entrails and intense and sudden swelling of the stomach.

11. Many are oppressed by a melancholy disposition. Some of them are so weakened that they do not wish either to speak or converse with people.

12. Many may have their eyes constricted, and the whole body, especially the face, almost completely suffused by a yellow or ashen color.

13. When witchcraft has by chance befallen the sick, he is generally attacked by some serious trouble, seized with fear and terror; if he is a boy, he immediately bewails himself and his eyes change to a dark color, and other perceptible changes are

observed. Wherefore the discrete exorcist takes care to disclose the recognized signs of this sort to the relatives and those present to avoid scandal.

14. It is especially significant if skilled physicians are not sure what the affliction is, and cannot form an opinion about it; or if the medications prescribed do not help but rather increase the sickness.

15. Sometimes the only indications of possession are considered circumstantial and inferential, as employing witchcraft for hatred, love, sterility, storm-raising, ligature, or harm to animals.

In another observation by Rouen (1644), we have the following indications of true possession:

1. To think oneself possessed.

2. To lead a wicked life.

3. To live outside the rules of society.

4. To be persistently ill, falling into heavy sleep and vomiting unusual objects (either natural objects: toads, serpents, worms, iron, stones, etc.; or artificial objects: nails, pins, etc., which may also be illusions caused by witches and not inevitably signs of possession by the devil).

5. To blaspheme.

6. To make a pact with the devil.

7. To be troubled with spirits (an absolute and inner possession and residence in the body of the person).

8. To show a frightening and horrible countenance.

9. To be tired of living.

10. To be uncontrollable and violent.

11. To make sounds and movements like an animal.

One Middle Ages demonologist, Pre Esprit de Bosroger, classified the signs of authentic possession in La Piete affligee . . . Saincte Elizabeth de Louviers:

1. Denial of knowledge of fits after the paroxysm has ended.

2. Incessant obscenities and blasphemies.

3. Circumstantial descriptions of the sabbat.

4. Fear of sacred relics and sacraments.

5. Violent cursing at any prayer.

6. Lewd exposure and acts of abnormal strength.

7. Similar manifestations in other demoniacs.

In Michael Dalton's Guide to Jurymen, seven signs of possession were explained:

1. When a healthful person shall be suddenly taken, and without probable reason, or natural cause appearing.

2. When two or more are taken in the like strange fits, in many things.

3. When the afflicted party in his fits tells truly many things, what other persons absent are doing or saying, and the like.

4. When the parties shall do many things strangely, or speak many

things to purpose, and yet out of their fits know not anything thereof.

5. When there is a strength supernatural, as that a strong man or two shall not be able to keep down a child, or weak person, upon a bed.

6. When the party vomits up crooked pins, needles, nails, coals, lead, straw, hair, or the like.

7. When the party shall see visibly some apparition, and shortly after some mischief shall befall him.

Medical Evaluation

One of the criticisms of alleged cases of possession is the tendency of many to blame the devil for every form of ill fortune or malady that afflicts the human condition. And rightfully so.

There are always circles of skepticism and credulosity in every age of the Church: On the one hand, many refuse to acknowledge that the devil or the demons are real spiritual beings who can and do interact with the human family; on the other hand, many imaginative people believe that the devil lurks around every corner and causes every evil incident in the world.

The former rationale usually comes from insecure liberal theologians who must find ways to demythologize the supernatural phenomena of Sacred Scripture. Perhaps this is their way of appearing different, imaginative, creative, or intellectual to their fellow colleagues or to others in the Church. The latter occurs among a variety of people who display inordinate fascination with the devil and all forms of evil: biblical fundamentalists; fire-and-brimstone preachers; those caught up in the wave of apocalypticism; or those who are highly influenced by ghost stories, demonic movies, or sensationalized books that deal with cases of possession and exorcism in the twentieth century.

Obviously, both extremes of skepticism and credulosity should be avoided when dealing with the topic of demonology and the spirits of darkness. The Church has spoken clearly on these matters many times in the past.

Of course, many more reported cases of diabolic oppression and possession occurred in past centuries than in our current era. Why is this so? Up until this past century, the worlds of science and medicine were really in their infancy compared with today's world of knowledge and technology.

Many illnesses or maladies in centuries past were mysterious and unexplainable to the then-known worlds of medicine and psychology. As a result, a number of the physiological, neurological, and psychological diseases that we know today were often attributed to demonic oppression or possession. Understandably, these were somewhat rational judgments at the time of their occurrence.

What else would a religious-minded, rational creature attribute to bizarre or unusual behavior that defied any known natural explanation?

It is precisely because of our deeper understanding of such illnesses or maladies that the Church today is more cautious about accepting diabolical phenomena such as oppression or possession. Although she still proclaims the reality of the devil and the possibility of diabolic oppression or possession, these claims are much rarer now; furthermore, the Church insists on very extensive examinations of the alleged victim before she will even consider a formal or solemn exorcism.

The other reason for this critical stand is obvious: The Church must maintain her credibility with the faithful, lest they be misled or deceived.

Finally, because the devil is the **great impostor**, deceiver, and liar, the Church must be very cautious and use the utmost discretion when dealing with claims that surround the Father of Lies. Although the evil spirit works best undetected, nevertheless if undue attention or panic is brought to the masses through false claims of diabolical attack or possession, the evil spirit gains a whole new advantage. Panic, fear, and confusion are tendencies that draw one away from Christian faith and peace.

Abnormal or excessive preoccupation with what appears to be the works of the devil sometimes causes one to fall right into his grip. There is often a fine line between focusing one's interest and attention on a particular phenomenon, then slowly becoming a part of that experience without even being aware that it has happened.

Satan's most powerful attacks are often subtle. Thus, great prudence and caution is always demanded by the Church.

Father de Tonquedec, S.J., former exorcist of the Paris diocese, wrote a book entitled Les maladies nerveuses ou mentales et les manifestations diaboliqueus. In that highly respected work, Father de Tonquedec describes a variety of illnesses that are common to both genuine cases of possession and those that have a medical or psychological basis. The validity of his study is clear: Because many of the signs or phenomena associated with the natural and preternatural worlds are often identical or at least they often share similar observable characteristics great care must be taken to avoid a premature judgment about authentic diabolical influence that may in fact have a natural, medical explanation after all.

What are some of the possible medical explanations behind alleged cases of diabolical possession? It might be helpful here to list a number of diseases or abnormalities associated with the human condition that may be responsible for phenomena that are very similar to those experienced during diabolical possession.

This recognition is important, for it encourages the Church not to make premature judgments about such phenomena until all natural explanations have been exhausted: namely, all medical and scientific explanations. Only then will we avoid the grave mistake of identifying particular people as oppressed or possessed when a natural explanation is in order. To make a false judgment about oppression or possession is not only emotionally and psychologically damaging to the suspected victim, it can also cause great harm and turmoil for the exorcist, his assistants, friends, and relatives of the
accused, not to mention the damage to the Church's credibility.

Conditions Often Mistaken
For Possession

ADAMS-STOKES SYNDROME Giddiness, fainting, sometimes

convulsions,resulting from slowed heart action caused by a heart block.

ANGINA A condition characterized by spastic attacks with sensations of strangling, pressure, or suffocation.

ANGIONEUROTIC EDEMA Acute local swelling, like giant hives under the skin, frequently a result of food allergy. The swelling can be very serious around the tongue and larynx, threatening suffocation.

ATAXIA Loss of muscle coordination. Degeneration of parts of the spinal cord, causing lightning pains, a staggering gait, disturbances of the eyes, bladder, and other organs.

BELL'S PALSY Paralysis of the facial nerve, usually temporary; it leaves the victim unable to move muscles of the mouth, eye, and forehead on one side of the face. The habit of grinding the teeth.

CATATONIA A phase of schizophrenia in which the patient stands or sits in some awkward position for hours on end and resists all attempts to get him to speak or move.

CAUSALGIA Excruciating, burning pain caused by injury to sensory nerves, especially of the palms and soles; often associated with poor circulation to the part and discoloration, clamminess, and coldness of the skin.

CEREBRAL PALSY A form of paralysis manifested by jerky, writhing, spastic movements, resulting from damage to brain-center controls of muscles.

CHOREA A disease of the nervous system manifested by involuntary, irregular, rapid, jerky movements of muscles of the face, legs, and arms.

CLONIC Spasmodic muscular contractions and relaxations that succeed each other alternately and jerkily.

DEAF-MUTISM Inability to hear and speak. The two disabilities are interrelated.

DELIRIUM A state of mental confusion, excitement, incoherent talk, restlessness, and hallucinations. Delirium may be associated with high fever, poisoning, drug intoxication, infections, and metabolic disturbances.

DELIRIUM TREMENS A serious, sometimes fatal, form of delirium, most often occurring in persons with a long history of alcoholism but occasionally associated with other poisonings of the brain cells, senile brain changes, and psychoses. The victim may have vivid visual hallucinations, often of moving colored animals he may actually see pink elephants but the hallucinated creatures may be very tiny and frequently he feels as well as sees them crawling over his skin. Anxiety, fear, trembling of the hands, mental confusion, and sleeplessness are other manifestations. Physical restraints may be necessary. The delirium lasts for a couple of days to a week or more and usually terminates in profound sleep. The patient is often malnourished and run down physically.

DERMATITIS Inflammation of the skin; often called eczema. Causes are varied, including chemicals, plants, household agents, cosmetics, drugs, X rays, and food.

ECCHYMOSIS Bleeding into the skin and discoloration of skin so produced, as, a back-and-blue bruise that fades from purple to green to yellow as blood trapped in tissues is absorbed.

ELEPHANTIASIS Gross enlargement of a body part (legs, scrotum) due to fluids in tissue spaces under the skin, dammed back by obstruction of lymphatic drainage channels.

EPILEPSY A nervous disorder of varying severity, marked by recurring explosive discharge of electrical activity of brain cells, producing convulsions, loss of consciousness, or brief clouding of consciousness.

EXFOLIATION Peeling or shedding of surface skin in scales or sheets.

EXOPHTHALMOS Bulging eyes, popping eyes, a condition characteristic of thyroid disease.

HUNTINGTON'S CHOREA A degenerative disease of the central nervous system that results from a dominant mutation. This disease may cause a change in character: One may become irritable, obstinate, and moody. Also evident is impairment of attention, memory, and judgment. A disorderliness of thought occurs, and the dementia may become extreme. Signs such as bodily twitching and bobbing movements are often observed, along with involuntary movements that are irregular and jerky. The muscles of the face may contract, resulting in grimaces while those of the tongue, lips, and respiratory muscles lead to a hesitating, explosive, poorly articulated speech that may be difficult to understand. The fingers may twitch, and the eyes may flutter. One suffering Huntington's disease may become violent or suicidal. The victim often neglects his appearance, refusing to bathe, to change, or to comb his hair.

JACKSONIAN SEIZURE An epileptic seizure that originates in a local part of the brain and whose effects are limited to one part of the body; for example, a twitching arm or leg.

JAUNDICE Yellowish discoloration of skin and tissues by bile pigments in the blood. The skin is usually very itchy and the urine dark yellow or brown. The whites of the eyes have a yellowish tinge; in skin discolorations that might be mistaken for jaundice, the whites of the eyes remain clear.

LEPROSY A chronic disease, often very painful, that inflicts cruel deformities and mutilations, caused by bacteria closely related to those that cause tuberculosis. About twelve million persons suffer from leprosy today. Symptoms include discoloration of the skin;

thick, knobby growths on the skin; grossly distorted features; and bodily parts such as fingers or toes that shrivel and eventually fall off.

LYMPHEDEMA Swelling of a part of the body, especially the legs or arms, from a backup of fluids because of obstruction or inadequacy of the lymphatic drainage system. The condition may cause enlargement of the part.

MALARIA An infectious disease characterized by chills and intermittent fever, caused by parasites transmitted to man by the bites of mosquitoes.

NARCOLEPSY Irresistible attacks of sleep, often with transient muscular weakness. Attacks occur during normal waking hours under all possible conditions. There are no signs of disease or abnormality.

NARCOSIS A state of deep sleep, unconsciousness, and insensibility to pain.

PARKINSON'S DISEASE A neurological disorder that involves a pathology of one part of the brain's motor system. Common symptoms may include muscular rigidity, irregular muscular movements, festination, scanning speech, mask like facial expressions, and drooling.

PSORIASIS A chronic disease of the skin that usually persists years with periods of remission and recurrence. Common symptoms include elevated lesions in various bodily parts, such as the scalp, knees, nails, and lower back. Psoriasis causes silvery scales to form on the skin that eventually drops off.

PSYCHOMOTOR SEIZURE A relatively mild form of epileptic attack that the victim never remembers. The person does not fall but may stagger, make restless movements and strange sounds, lose contact with his environment for a moment or two.

REYE'S SYNDROME A serious viral disease of children that occurs about a week after recovery from a viral infection such as the flu. Symptoms of violent vomiting, hallucinations, and wild behavior have been reported.

SCLERODERMA Hidebound skin: a connective tissue disease of unknown cause. The first signs usually appear in the skin of the hands and feet, in patchy areas that gradually involve more and more of the body. The skin slowly becomes hard, thickened, stiff, smooth, and shiny. The face may become masklike because of the loss of flexibility.

TICS Habitual spasms that are quick, twitchy, repetitive movements of certain muscle groups, always in the same manner: pouting the lips; batting the eyelids; wrinkling the nose; making faces; shaking the head; shrugging the shoulders; tilting the neck; etc. Tics usually develop during childhood and often disappear as the child grows older.

TOURETTE'S SYNDROME A tic syndrome involving the upper body, including the face, shoulders, and arms. Common symptoms of those afflicted with Tourette's syndrome are excessive blinking, frowning, grimacing, sniffing, grunting, swallowing, head twisting, coughing, grunting, or explosive verbalizations that may include filthy outbursts of language.

TRENCH MOUTH Painful, swollen, malodorous inflammation of the mouth and gums.

TRICHOTILLOMANIA A neurotic habit of pulling out one's own hair.

Other Factors To Consider

What are some of the mental diseases or malfunctions that are taken into consideration during an investigation of an alleged demonic oppression or possession? It might be appropriate to list a number of them here, for it has been proven many times in cases of false diabolical oppression and possession that one of the following was the cause of such strange behavior.

ANTISOCIAL Exhibiting attitudes and overt behavior contrary to accepted customs, standards, and moral principles of society.

ANXIETY A normal reaction to a problem or situation and a psychic affliction; in the latter, the source of apprehension cannot be identified by the subject and the anxiety is the outward expression of an inner fear.

CATALEPSY A psychogenic attack resulting in a loss of voluntary motion accompanied by stupor.

CLAUSTROPHOBIA A morbid fear of confinement or of entering small places.

COMPULSION Neurotic, repetitive, stereotyped, and irrepressible activity that is the motor expression of obsessive thinking.

COPROLALIA Uncontrolled utterance of obscene words or phrases; commonly encountered in patients suffering from schizophrenia and the obsessive-compulsive reaction.

CYCLOTHYMIA A cycle of emotional variation in moods, of a milder form than the manic-depressive reaction.

DELIRIUM An acute mental disturbance characterized by confusion, excitement, and disorientation, and not infrequently, by hallucinations and abject fear.

DELUSION A belief arising without external stimulus and contrary to fact, as a delusion of grandeur, of persecution, etc. It is psychogenic in origin.

DEMENTIA Mental deterioration, usually implying serious impairment of intellect, irrationality, confusion, stupor, an insane behavior. Dementia may result from poisons, physical changes in the brain, toxins produced by disease, or psychoses of which the basic cause is unknown.

DEPERSONALIZATION Loss of the sense of personal identity, usually accompanied by feelings of unreality about the environment or oneself.

DISORIENTATION Loss of the ability to place oneself in relation to time, place, or person.

ECHOLALIA Irresistible repetition of a word or phrase heard; common in schizophrenia.

EXHIBITIONISM A morbid desire to reveal parts of the body that are customarily concealed.

HALLUCINATION An impression not based on true sensory perception; it may involve distortions of any or all of the five senses; a common symptom in several forms of mental disorder.

HYPERPROSEXIA A form of obsessive-compulsive reaction in which the subject is absorbed by one idea to the exclusion of all others.

HYPOMANIA A milder form of the manic phase of manic-depressive psychosis; restlessness, distractibility, and flight of ideas are observed.

HYSTERIA A psychoneurotic disorder arising from an emotional conflict, in which repressed material finds an outlet through sensorimotor disturbances, such as blindness, loss of certain sensations, and paralysis of the limbs, with loss or impairment of speech function.

KAINOPHOBIA Morbid fear of new things, persons, or situations.

KORSAKOFF'S PSYCHOSIS A severe mental disturbance that

usually follows a bout of delirium. Symptoms may include a loss of memory for recent weeks, or a falsification of memory. The psychosis is associated with chronic alcoholism and chronic malnutrition.

LOGORRHEA Uncontrolled and continuous speech, usually repetitious but coherent.

MANIC-DEPRESSIVE PSYCHOSIS An affective psychosis in which the symptoms are predominantly expressed in emotional outbursts or apathy, hyperactivity, elation or depression, often with mood swings between the extremes of these characteristics.

MELANCHOLIA Profound sadness; morbid grief, or grief that outlives a reasonable duration.

NIHILISTIC DELUSION A delusion, encountered in schizophrenia, that the environment, or large elements of it, have vanished, often expressed in the following ideas: There is no more people, The earth has disintegrated, Life has ceased, and similar pronouncements.

PARAMNESIA Confusion over the details of past experiences, often exhibited as the inability to separate reality from fantasy.

PARANOIA A form of mental illness characterized by suspiciousness, delusions, feelings of being persecuted, spied upon, endangered. The victim's delusions are so systematized and seemingly logical that they can be quite convincing to others, especially since the paranoid victim often seems quite sane and reasonable except on one or a few subjects.

PHOBIA A morbid, abnormal fear, usually without adequate cause.

PSYCHONEUROSIS Emotionally based disturbance of the personality, often severe enough to be handicapping, generally a defensive reaction to psychic threats and conflicts.

PSYCHOPATH An older term used to describe a sociopath, a person suffering from a character disorder.

PSYCHOSIS A major mental disorder principally characterized by deviant, often bizarre, behavior and withdrawal from the normal stream of life; some of the symptoms commonly present are regression, hallucinations, delusions, disorientation, and verbalization of aberrant ideas.

PSYCHOSOMATIC DISEASE Disability, sometimes but not always without accompanying physical causes, in which the disturbing emotions of the person play an important part in inciting, worsening, or continuing the disability.

SCHIZOPHRENIA A major psychosis, characterized by introversion, regression, childishness, asocial (possibly antisocial) behavior, hallucinations, delusions, depersonalization, and aberrant ideas.

SCOPOPHOBIA Pathological fear of being seen; a scopophobiac will insists that window shades be drawn, or may keep his eyes tightly closed; it is a common sign of schizophrenia.

SOCIOPATH One who suffers from a character disorder as manifested by the inability to conform to acceptable social behavior. Nonconforming behavior may be antisocial, amoral, or sexually deviant.

SPLIT PERSONALITY Also known as a multiple personality, a rare character disorder whereby distinct individual personality types exist within the same person. One personality may dominate or take over at a particular time, followed by another at a later time. The cause of multiple personalities is unknown; however, prior emotional distress or trauma may have triggered a series of repressive personality types that become activated from time to time. This activation serves as a defense mechanism, allowing that person to cope with his or her environment or with other people who may appear as a threat.

This is not to say that all abnormal behavior or phenomena must be physiological or psychological in origin, even if the signs are present to the investigating experts. It must be realized that the evil spirit also uses signs and phenomena that are very similar to those found in cases of mental disturbances or diseases. Thus, it is often difficult to tell whether the phenomenon is caused by a diabolical spirit or by a mental or neurological abnormality in the one who is examined. Sometimes the evil spirit uses physiological diseases to hide behind his own oppressive actions.

Thus, there could be present in the victim both a natural cause and a preternatural cause of the disturbances. For this reason, both the Church and the world of science must work together and not disregard any possible diagnosis until all factors have been investigated and verified to the best of all practical knowledge.

If there has been any weakness or fault in both circles, this would be it: to ignore any possible alternative explanation merely because it doesn't fit with the known or agree with one's background, training, or experiences. Such foolish attitudes embarrassed many closed-minded people of the past: those who insisted that the world was flat; those who believed that the universe was created in 4000 B.C.; those who thought that epilepsy was demonic possession; those who claimed that the earth was the center of the universe; and those who refuse to believe in the reality of the devil or in diabolical oppression and possession!

Commentary On
The Roman Ritual

Prelude

Exorcism is a practice dating back to ancient times. A pagan witch doctor is to sorcery what a Christian exorcist is to an exorcism. In every tribe, culture, or society both primitive and modern, one can find evidence of beliefs in demons or evil spirits.

These beliefs include oppression, possession, and exorcism as means of ridding the evil spirit from the body or surrounding environment. It is clear that various types of exorcisms are not limited to the traditional beliefs and practices of the Roman Catholic Church. However, Catholic exorcism involves the expulsion of demons or devils. Many religions believe in various gods, devils, and witches, so the Catholic position is exclusive to her theological tradition.

The original **Roman Ritual** was written in 1614 during the pontificate of Pope Paul V (1605-1621) and first published by Maximilian von Eynatten. In all actuality, the text was developed over a long period of Church history. The belief in the possibility of possession and exorcism dates back to Jesus in the Gospels. This tradition continued through the Middle Ages and was finally formalized by the seventeenth century.

In 1626, another, far more comprehensive guide was published concerning these beliefs and practices concerning the rite of Catholic exorcism. This 1,232-page book, **Thesaurus Exorcismorum**, detailed all possible signs of authentic diabolical oppression and possession, with suggested remedies or actions for each phenomenon.

Although the official exorcism manual for the universal Church was still the Roman Ritual, nevertheless the Thesaurus Exorcismorum influenced the Church's knowledge about evil spirits and exorcism practices.

During this time period, the theologians of the day often referred to the invading demon as the **maleficium**: literally, the harmful or evil one. In turn, maleficia was a word sometimes used to describe the various misfortunes, injuries, or calamities suffered by souls who were oppressed or possessed by evil spirits (although this term was also used to refer to the spells or hexes performed on another by witches or sorcerers).

Another manual was published in 1720 that served as a guideline for dealing with possession and exorcism. This was called the **Manual of Exorcism**, originally translated from a Spanish manuscript.

Thus, the Roman Catholic Church did not suddenly devise an exorcism rite as a reaction to an overly superstitious era. The tradition has slowly developed since the time of Christ Himself, who gave witness to the reality of such spiritual matters. Such an honored practice was exorcism that the primitive Church made it one of the four minor orders. As early as the second century, St. Justin Martyr (100-165) had this to say in his Apology: For many of our Christian men exorcised numberless demoniacs throughout the whole world and in the city of Rome in the name of Jesus Christ. . . . They have healed and do heal them, rendering the possessing devils helpless and driving them out of the men, who could not be cured by all the other exorcists or by those who used incantations and drugs.

Since the seventeenth century, the Roman Ritual has been used in innumerable solemn exorcisms sanctioned by the Church. In 1947, revisions were made to the original text. (Francis Cardinal Spellman wrote the introduction to this newly revised rite.)

Summary of the
Roman Ritual of Exorcism

The following information is a comprehensive commentary on the traditional Roman Ritual of the Catholic Church. This rite remained in effect from 1614 until recently, when it was revised. It is interesting to note that there never has been an official English translation of the text; rather, the Latin version remains the only officially authorized rite of the Church. The actual rite is not to be used by anyone other than a qualified priest who is authorized by his bishop to perform a **solemn exorcism** in the name of the Church.

The reason for this is obvious: An unauthorized person runs the risk of serious harm to himself or to others involved with authentic cases of obsession or possession. Without the proper authority to perform exorcisms, and without the prayerful support of the Church, one may be exposing himself to dangerous diabolic attacks. These attacks often injure people.

Preliminary Considerations
For the Exorcist

1. A bishop must authorize a particular priest to perform a solemn exorcism in the name of the Church. This priest should be wise and prudent. This will help him in his role as exorcist. An experienced priest of mature age is usually sought, although this is not always the case. Knowledge and education are also desired. The priest should be a man of learning, one who has studied various works on demonology and knows the activities and characteristics of the demon quite well. Above all, the exorcist must be a humble man of great faith and piety.

2. It is important that an exorcist not be too readily persuaded that a reported case of demonic possession is authentic. (Refer also to

number 5, below.) Rather, he must use great caution and prudence when investigating such matters. In order to establish that an authentic case of diabolical obsession or possession has taken place, a series of signs are looked for: speaking in unknown languages or understanding unknown languages; when the victim knows about things that are distant or hidden; when he shows a physical strength far exceeding his age or normal condition. These have been traditionally accepted as **signs of authentic diabolical possession**, although others are considered as well. Usually, a combination of all these signs point to a demonic presence.

3. The exorcist is helped in his discernment by asking the victim what effects are felt in his or her own body: unexplainable and uncontrollable urges or impulses to lust, drink, shout obscenities, etc.; unusual twitches, bodily spasms, changes in one's face or eyes; feelings of severe depression or suicidal tendencies when none were present before; a heavy pressure of weighing down of the body by an unseen force; physical blows, slaps, hair pulling, or bruises caused by unseen forces; and so on.

4. By examining and questioning the victim, an exorcist is encouraged to pay close attention to the tactics of the evil spirit: when he manifests himself; how he makes himself known; whether any particular signs, words, actions, or prayers aggravate the evil spirit. Above all, the exorcist must carefully discern whatever the demonic spirit says through the possessed victim. It is often difficult to tell whether the spirit is lying or not; the devil often mixes lies with the truth and utilizes the device of trickery and deception.

5. The exorcist must not automatically assume that diabolical possession has not occurred just because no visible or audible signs of possession are present. The evil spirit often hides his presence in order to avoid a confrontation with the exorcist. Even when the demon shows himself and later appears to have left after the completion of an exorcism, the exorcist must not always presume that the spirit is really gone. And if the diabolic being has departed, it is possible for him to return and repossess the victim. It is worth noting that there may have been more than one spirit

possessing the victim.

6. The exorcist must look for signs that encouraged the evil spirit to enter the victim in the first place: spells, curses, the practice of witchcraft or magic, engaging in seances, conjuring forces from the spiritual world, etc. If one of these sources can be determined, the exorcist may make use of special prayers that invite the possessed victim to renounce Satan in the name of Jesus.

7. According to Jesus, there are some evil spirits that cannot be expelled except when the exorcist engages in fasting and prayer.

8. The ideal place to perform the exorcism is in a church or in the home of the possessed victim. In church, the demon is often weakened by the presence of holy objects, relics, holy water, and the cross. If this is not possible, then the victim's home is the next logical choice. There, the possessed victim is in familiar surroundings, is more comfortable, and may have family present for support and for prayer. Because the demon is often attached to a certain place or environment, it may be a good idea to confront the evil spirit directly at the place where he will most likely resist leaving. Many sessions may be needed with the one possessed.

9. The exorcist should encourage the victim to prepare for the exorcism through prayer and fasting. He should build up the victim's confidence and will to resist the spirits of darkness. Above all, the exorcist should strengthen the victim's faith and prepare him for a difficult and dangerous battle through continued trust in the name and power of Jesus. On the other hand, he should not frighten the individual. The encouragement he should give the possessed is not always possible, due to the condition of the possessed.

10. The possessed victim is encouraged to wear or hold a crucifix during the exorcism. Relics of the saints may be placed on the victim's chest, bed, or a nearby table. But let care be taken that these holy things are not treated irreverently and damaged by the evil spirit. The Holy Eucharist should not be placed on the head or

anywhere on the body of the possessed. There is a danger that it will be treated irreverently.

11. The exorcist must not make great speeches or question the diabolical spirit out of mere curiosity, particularly concerning future events and hidden matters that have nothing to do with his work. He should command the unclean spirit to keep silent and only to respond to what is asked of him.

12. Questions the exorcist must ask the possessing evil spirit are, for example, the number and name of the possessing spirits, when they entered the possessed, and why they entered him. The exorcist should attempt to restrain all vanities, mockeries, and foolishness of the evil spirit. He should treat them with contempt. And he should admonish those who are present who should be few in number not to take notice of what the evil spirit says and not to put any questions to the possessed. Those who are present will normally pray humbly and fervently to God for the deliverance of the possessed.

13. The exorcist should perform and read the exorcism with command, authority, great faith, humility, and fervor. And, when he sees that the possessing spirit is being disturbed or tortured, he should multiply all these efforts in order to break down the will of the entity. If he sees some part of the possessed person's body moving or pierced or some swelling appearing, the exorcist should periodically make the Sign of the Cross and sprinkle holy water on the victim.

14. The exorcist needs to pay attention to the words and expressions that disturb the evil spirit most, and repeat them very often. And when he arrives at the point of expulsion, he repeats the command to depart, always increasing the punishment. And, if he sees that he is succeeding, he must persevere until he is finally victorious.

15. The exorcist must be careful not to offer any medicine to the possessed or suggest any to him. All this he should leave to the

medical doctors.

16. If he is exorcising a woman, he should have with him some reputable women who will hold the possessed when she is tormented and shaken by the evil spirit. Such women should be of great patience and belong to the family of the possessed. The exorcist must be mindful of scandal and avoid doing or saying anything that could provoke ill for himself or for others.

17. During exorcism, the exorcist should use the words of the Bible rather than his own or somebody else's. Also, he should command the evil spirit to state whether he is kept within the possessed because of some magical spell. If the possessed has within him
something with a spell on it, he must vomit it up. If it is outside his body in some place or another, the evil spirit must tell the exorcist where it is. When the exorcist finds it, he must burn it, praying all the while.

18. If the possessed person is freed from the evil spirit, he should be advised to avoid sinful actions and thoughts. If he does not, he could give the evil spirit a fresh occasion for returning and possessing him. In that case, he could be in a much worse condition than before.

Preparation for Solemn Exorcism

When a solemn exorcism is about to begin, the priest appointed by the bishop as exorcist must make a number of preparations. Before or on the appointed day, he is recommended to fast, go to confession, say Mass, and ask for God's protection and mercy. The exorcist's clothing is determined by tradition: Normally, he wears a long black garment with surplice and purple stole.

All detached objects in the room should be removed to avoid the danger of items being thrown at the participants during the ritual of exorcism. Normally, one small table is placed by the side of the possessed victim. The following may be placed on the table: a Bible, holy water, candles, and perhaps a relic or picture of a favorite saint of the victim. If the Eucharist is present, it should be safely guarded to avoid any irreverent act on the part of the demon.

Then the priest must say a **prayer for protection** of all who will be present during the exorcism: his assistants, the victim, and himself. Holy water is sprinkled on those who are present at this time.

Next, a series of invocations are performed, followed by responses from the assistants. The priest reads from **The Litanies of the Saints**, which is followed by an Our Father from the assistants. Psalm 53 is read next by the exorcist. Then a series of prayers are spoken asking God to protect the victim and deliverance from the forces of evil.

During these series of prayers, the evil spirit is referred to by a host of names that are symbolic of its attributes or characteristics: the Enemy, Son of Iniquity, Roaring Lion, Beast, Serpent, Unclean Spirit, etc.

Then the exorcist demands the evil spirit to reveal his identity and to disclose when he will depart forever. A series of Gospel readings may be said at this time: John 1:1-12, Mark 16:15-18, Luke 10:17-20, and Luke 11:14-22 are often used.

The priest then invokes the power of almighty God to subdue the forces of darkness. He prays for the strength to expel the evil spirit that is present in the victim. Particularly powerful is the invocation of the Holy Spirit to come to his assistance.

Next, the exorcist makes the Sign of the Cross and lays the tip of his purple stole on the neck or head of the possessed, while placing his right hand on the victim. He then commands the evil spirit to depart through the power of the cross of the Lord and in the holy name of Jesus. Throughout this time, the assistants present make various responses for each of the exorcist's prayers and commands.

In the next phase of the exorcism the priest commands the evil spirit to leave the victim by invoking numerous references to his name: Seducer, Satan, Unclean Spirit, Enemy, Robber, Traitor, Ancient Serpent, etc. During this phase, the Sign of the Cross is used several dozen times at critical points of the confrontation, even on the chest and forehead of the possessed victim.

Then the exorcist asks for the heavenly intercession of the following: God the Father, God the Son, God the Holy Spirit, Sts. Peter and Paul, the confessors, and all the saints and martyrs.

The exorcist speaks of the many times when the evil spirit had been expelled or defeated through confrontations with various biblical personalities: King Saul, Judas Iscariot, Simon the Magician, Ananias and Saphira, Elymas, and the Prophetess of Python. During this confrontational phase with the evil spirit, numerous prayers are often employed against the powers of darkness: the Pater Noster, the Ave Maria, the Credo, the Magnificat, and the Benedictus Canticle (ending the last two with a Gloria).

If it is necessary, the exorcist may have to perform the above procedures many times to finally expel the demon.

It is not uncommon for the one possessed to need many sessions in order to be delivered. Perhaps there are many spirits invading the body; it is also known that some demons are more powerful and resistant than others.

The next step involves recitation of the Profession of Faith. Particularly popular is the traditional version by St. Athanasius. This prayer proclaims the glory of the Trinity: God the Father, God the Son, and God the Holy Spirit. It also proclaims the divine mystery of God made flesh in Jesus Christ our Lord.

Finally, a reading of the Psalms is encouraged (such as 90, 67, 34, 30, 21, 3, 10, 12), followed by a prayer of thanksgiving.

This final prayer asks of God to protect the released victim from repossession by the invading spirit. The priest asks that God's love and peace enter the victim in place of the departed darkness.

A rite for the exorcism of places involves expelling the spirits of darkness from homes, particular places, or specific environments. It is performed by the diocesan bishop himself, or by a priest whom he has officially appointed. Whenever an exorcism is performed on a place, the sprinkling of holy water is practiced regularly.

A common prayer that the faithful say is often used to seek protection from demonic spirits. It has been used in private exorcisms or in cases of diabolical obsession or partial possession. Because this traditional prayer is not an exclusive part of the Roman Rite of Exorcism but is permitted to be used by the faithful at large, it is repeated here:

The Prayer of Michael the Archangel

Most glorious Prince of the Heavenly Army, Holy Michael the Archangel, defend us in battle against the princes and powers and rulers of darkness in this world, against the spiritual iniquities of those former angels. Come to the help of men whom God made in his own image and whom he bought from the tyranny of Satan at a great price. The Church venerates you as her custodian and patron. The Lord confided to your care all the souls of those redeemed, so that you would lead them to happiness in Heaven. Pray to the God of peace that he crush Satan under our feet; so that Satan no longer be able to hold men captive and thus injure the Church. Offer our prayers to the Most High God, so that his mercies be given us soon. Make captive that Animal, that Ancient serpent, which is enemy and evil spirit, and reduce it to everlasting nothingness, so that it no longer seduce the nations.

If you found this book to be informative, please leave a comment! Just go to the bottom of the following page link to express your thoughts. Thanks!

http://www.amazon.com/gp/product/B0190U6D60?*Version*=1&*entries*=0

My other published ebooks are on my Amazon Author Central page:

http://www.amazon.com/-/e/B001KIZJS4

BOOKS OF THE BIBLE
(In Alphabetical Order)

Old Testament

1 Chr / 1 Chronicles
2 Chr / 2 Chronicles
1 Kgs / 1 Kings
2 Kgs / 2 Kings
1 Mc / 2 Maccabees
1 Mc / 2 Maccabees
1 Sm / 1 Samuel
2 Sm / 2 Samuel
Am / Amos
Bar / Baruch
Dn / Daniel
Dt / Deuteronomy
Eccl / Ecclesiastes
Est / Esther
Ex / Exodus
Ez / Ezekiel
Ezr / Ezra
Gn / Genesis
Hb / Habakkuk
Hg / Haggai
Hos / Hosea
Is / Isaiah
Jer / Jeremiah
Jb / Job
Jl / Joel
Jon / Jonah
Jos / Joshua
Jgs / Judges
Jdt / Judith
Lam / Lamentations

Lv / Leviticus
Mal / Malachi
Mi / Micah
Na / Nahum
Neh / Nehemiah
Nm / Numbers
Ob / Obadiah
Prv / Proverbs
Ps(s) / Psalms
Ru / Ruth
Sir / Sirach
Sg / Song of Solomon
Tb / Tobit
Wis / Wisdom
Zec / Zechariah
Zep / Zephaniah

New Testament

1 Cor / 2 Corinthians
1 Cor / 2 Corinthians
1 Jn / 1 John
2 Jn / 2 John
3 Jn / 3 John
1 Pt / 1 Peter
2 Pt / 2 Peter
1 Thes / 1 Thessalonians
2 Thes / 2 Thessalonians
1 Tm / 1 Timothy
2 Tm / 2 Timothy
Acts / Acts of the Apostles
Col / Colossians
Eph / Ephesians
Gal / Galatians

Heb / Hebrews
Jas / James
Lk / Luke
Mk / Mark
Mt / Matthew
Phlm / Philemon
Phil / Philippians
Rom / Romans
Rv / Revelation
Ti / Titus

Printed in Great Britain
by Amazon

11611001R00058